COMPLETE CYBERSECURITY EXPERTISE

A Whole Cybersecurity Course

Manuh

CONTENTS

INTRODUCTION

In today's interconnected world, cybersecurity is more critical than ever before. With the rapid advancement of technology, the proliferation of internet-connected devices, and the increasing reliance on digital platforms for business, communication, and daily life, the potential for cyber threats has grown exponentially. From large multinational corporations to small and medium-sized enterprises (SMEs), from government agencies to educational institutions, and from financial services to healthcare providers, no organization or individual is immune to the risks posed by cyberattacks.

The consequences of cyber incidents can be devastating, ranging from financial losses and operational disruptions to reputational damage and legal liabilities. Data breaches can expose sensitive information, leading to identity theft, fraud, and a loss of trust among customers and stakeholders. Ransomware attacks can cripple critical infrastructure, halt business operations, and demand hefty ransoms for the return of encrypted data. Phishing schemes and social engineering tactics can exploit human vulnerabilities, bypassing technical defenses and compromising systems.

As the threat landscape continues to evolve, so too must the strategies and measures employed to safeguard against these dangers. This book, "Complete Cybersecurity Expertise," is designed to equip readers with a comprehensive understanding of cybersecurity principles, best practices, and emerging trends. It delves into the multifaceted aspects of cybersecurity, offering insights into protecting various sectors, from cloud environments and IoT devices to critical infrastructure and smart cities.

The chapters within this book provide in-depth knowledge and practical guidance on a wide range of topics, including cloud security, ethical hacking and penetration testing, incident response and forensics, securing emerging technologies, and the intersection of cybersecurity and artificial intelligence. Each chapter is crafted to address specific challenges and provide actionable solutions, empowering readers to enhance their cybersecurity posture and stay ahead of evolving threats.

Moreover, this book emphasizes the importance of building a cybersecurity culture within organizations, fostering leadership in cybersecurity, and navigating the complexities of compliance and regulatory requirements. By understanding the unique challenges faced by different industries and adopting tailored cybersecurity strategies, readers can better protect their digital assets, ensure business continuity, and maintain trust in an increasingly digital world.

In an era where digital transformation is reshaping industries and driving innovation, the role of cybersecurity cannot be overstated. This book serves as a valuable resource for cybersecurity professionals, IT practitioners, business leaders, and anyone interested in gaining expertise in the field of cybersecurity. As we embark on this journey to explore the intricacies of cybersecurity, let us remember that vigilance, adaptability, and continuous learning are key to staying secure in the ever-changing digital landscape.

CHAPTER 1: INTRODUCTION TO CYBERSECURITY

Overview of Cybersecurity

Cybersecurity is the practice of protecting systems, networks, and data from digital attacks. As technology becomes increasingly integrated into every aspect of our lives, the need for robust cybersecurity measures has never been more critical. Cybersecurity encompasses a wide range of strategies, technologies, and practices designed to safeguard digital assets from unauthorized access, damage, or theft.

Importance of Cybersecurity in the Modern World

In today's digital age, almost every facet of our personal and professional lives relies on interconnected systems and the internet. This dependency introduces various vulnerabilities that cybercriminals are eager to exploit. The consequences of cyberattacks can be devastating, affecting individuals, businesses, and governments alike. Here are some reasons why cybersecurity is paramount:

1. **Protecting Sensitive Information:** Personal data, financial information, and intellectual property must be safeguarded to prevent identity theft, financial loss, and competitive disadvantage.

2. **Ensuring Business Continuity:** Cyberattacks can disrupt operations, leading to downtime, loss of revenue, and damage to reputation. Effective

cybersecurity measures help ensure that businesses can continue to operate smoothly.

3. **Maintaining National Security:** Critical infrastructure, including power grids, transportation systems, and communication networks, are potential targets for cyberattacks. Securing these assets is essential for national security.

4. **Complying with Regulations:** Various laws and regulations mandate the protection of certain types of information. Non-compliance can result in hefty fines and legal consequences.

Key Concepts and Terminology

To understand cybersecurity, it is essential to familiarize yourself with some fundamental concepts and terminology:

1. **Threats:** Any potential danger to information or systems. Threats can be internal or external, malicious or accidental.

2. **Vulnerabilities:** Weaknesses or flaws in a system that can be exploited by threats to gain unauthorized access or cause harm.

3. **Risk:** The potential for loss or damage when a threat exploits a vulnerability. Risk is typically assessed based on the likelihood and impact of an event.

4. **Attack:** An attempt to exploit a vulnerability to achieve unauthorized access or cause harm. Attacks can vary in complexity and intent.

5. **Defense:** Measures and controls implemented to protect against threats and attacks. This includes technologies, policies, and practices.

History and Evolution of Cybersecurity

The concept of cybersecurity has evolved significantly over the past few decades. Here is a brief overview of its history:

1. **1960s - 1970s: Early Days of Computer Security:**

- The focus was primarily on physical security and access control to mainframe computers.
- Passwords and basic encryption methods were used to protect data.

2. **1980s: Emergence of Viruses and Hackers:**
   - The first computer viruses and worms were developed, leading to increased awareness of cybersecurity threats.
   - Hacking became more prevalent, and the term "cybersecurity" began to take shape.

3. **1990s: Growth of the Internet:**
   - The widespread adoption of the internet introduced new vulnerabilities and attack vectors.
   - Firewalls and antivirus software became essential tools for protecting systems.

4. **2000s: Advanced Threats and Regulations:**
   - Cybercriminals became more sophisticated, using techniques like phishing, malware, and ransomware.
   - Governments and organizations began implementing comprehensive cybersecurity frameworks and regulations.

5. **2010s - Present: Rise of Advanced Technologies:**
   - The advent of cloud computing, mobile devices, and the Internet of Things (IoT) brought new challenges and opportunities for cybersecurity.
   - Artificial intelligence (AI) and machine learning are now being leveraged to enhance threat detection and response.

Cybersecurity Threat Landscape

The threat landscape in cybersecurity is constantly evolving. Understanding the different types of threats is crucial for developing effective defense strategies. Here are some common cybersecurity threats:

1. **Malware:**
   - **Definition:** Malicious software designed to damage, disrupt, or gain unauthorized access to systems.
   - **Examples:** Viruses, worms, trojans, ransomware, spyware.

2. **Phishing:**
   - **Definition:** A social engineering attack where attackers impersonate legitimate entities to trick individuals into revealing sensitive information.
   - **Examples:** Phishing emails, spear-phishing, whaling.

3. **Denial-of-Service (DoS) and Distributed Denial-of-Service (DDoS) Attacks:**
   - **Definition:** Attacks that overwhelm a system or network with excessive traffic, rendering it unavailable to users.
   - **Examples:** Botnets, amplification attacks.

4. **Man-in-the-Middle (MitM) Attacks:**
   - **Definition:** Attacks where the attacker intercepts and manipulates communication between two parties without their knowledge.
   - **Examples:** Eavesdropping, session hijacking.

5. **Advanced Persistent Threats (APTs):**
   - **Definition:** Prolonged and targeted attacks where attackers gain unauthorized access and remain undetected for an extended period.

- ○ **Examples:** State-sponsored attacks, cyber espionage.
6. **Insider Threats:**
  - ○ **Definition:** Threats originating from within the organization, typically involving employees or contractors who misuse their access privileges.
  - ○ **Examples:** Data theft, sabotage.

Conclusion

In this chapter, we have introduced the fundamental concepts of cybersecurity, its importance in the modern world, and the evolving threat landscape. As we delve deeper into the subsequent chapters, we will explore various aspects of cybersecurity, including risk management, security policies, network security, and more. By understanding these concepts and practices, you will be better equipped to protect digital assets and navigate the ever-changing world of cybersecurity.

CHAPTER 2: UNDERSTANDING CYBER THREATS

Overview

The digital landscape is rife with various types of cyber threats that pose significant risks to individuals, businesses, and governments. Understanding these threats is crucial for developing effective cybersecurity strategies and defenses. This chapter delves into the different types of cyber threats, their attack vectors, the motivations behind them, and notable case studies that illustrate their impact.

Types of Cyber Threats

1. **Malware:**
   - **Definition:** Malware, short for malicious software, is any software intentionally designed to cause damage to a computer, server, client, or network.
   - **Types of Malware:**
     - **Viruses:** Malicious programs that attach themselves to legitimate files and spread when the files are shared.
     - **Worms:** Self-replicating malware that spreads without user intervention, often exploiting network vulnerabilities.

- **Trojans:** Malicious programs disguised as legitimate software that grant unauthorized access to attackers.
- **Ransomware:** Malware that encrypts a victim's files and demands payment for the decryption key.
- **Spyware:** Software that secretly monitors and collects user information without consent.
- **Adware:** Software that displays unwanted advertisements, often bundled with free software.
- **Examples:** WannaCry ransomware, Zeus trojan, Stuxnet worm.

2. **Phishing:**
   - **Definition:** Phishing is a social engineering attack in which attackers impersonate legitimate entities to trick individuals into revealing sensitive information.
   - **Types of Phishing:**
     - **Email Phishing:** Fraudulent emails that appear to come from reputable sources, asking recipients to click on malicious links or provide personal information.
     - **Spear Phishing:** Targeted phishing attacks aimed at specific individuals or organizations, often using personalized information to increase credibility.
     - **Whaling:** Phishing attacks targeting high-profile individuals, such as executives or government officials.

- **Smishing:** Phishing attacks conducted via SMS messages.
- **Vishing:** Phishing attacks conducted via voice calls.
  - **Examples:** The 2016 Democratic National Committee (DNC) email breach, PayPal phishing emails, IRS tax scam calls.

3. **Denial-of-Service (DoS) and Distributed Denial-of-Service (DDoS) Attacks:**
   - **Definition:** DoS attacks involve overwhelming a target system or network with excessive traffic, rendering it unavailable to users. DDoS attacks amplify this effect by using multiple compromised systems to launch the attack.
   - **Techniques:**
     - **Flood Attacks:** Sending a high volume of traffic to overwhelm the target's bandwidth.
     - **Amplification Attacks:** Exploiting vulnerable systems to generate large response traffic towards the target.
     - **SYN Flood Attacks:** Exploiting the TCP handshake process to consume server resources.
   - **Examples:** The 2016 Dyn DNS DDoS attack, the 2000 Yahoo! DoS attack, the Mirai botnet attack.

4. **Man-in-the-Middle (MitM) Attacks:**
   - **Definition:** In MitM attacks, attackers intercept and manipulate communication between two parties without their knowledge.
   - **Techniques:**

- **Eavesdropping:** Intercepting and listening to communication between parties.
- **Session Hijacking:** Taking control of a user's session after successful authentication.
- **SSL Stripping:** Downgrading HTTPS connections to HTTP to intercept data.
  ◦ **Examples:** The 2011 DigiNotar breach, Wi-Fi eavesdropping attacks, compromised routers intercepting banking transactions.

5. **Advanced Persistent Threats (APTs):**
   ◦ **Definition:** APTs are prolonged and targeted cyberattacks where attackers gain unauthorized access and remain undetected for an extended period, often sponsored by nation-states.
   ◦ **Phases of APTs:**
     - **Initial Compromise:** Gaining access through phishing, malware, or exploiting vulnerabilities.
     - **Establishing Foothold:** Deploying backdoors and persistent malware.
     - **Escalating Privileges:** Gaining higher levels of access within the network.
     - **Internal Reconnaissance:** Mapping the network and identifying valuable assets.
     - **Data Exfiltration:** Stealing sensitive information and transmitting it to external servers.
     - **Maintaining Persistence:** Ensuring continued access despite detection

  attempts.
- ◦ **Examples:** Stuxnet, APT28 (Fancy Bear), APT29 (Cozy Bear).

6. **Insider Threats:**
   - ◦ **Definition:** Insider threats originate from within the organization, typically involving employees or contractors who misuse their access privileges.
   - ◦ **Types of Insider Threats:**
     - ▪ **Malicious Insiders:** Employees with malicious intent, such as stealing data or sabotaging systems.
     - ▪ **Negligent Insiders:** Employees who unintentionally cause harm through careless actions or lack of awareness.
     - ▪ **Compromised Insiders:** Employees whose accounts have been compromised by external attackers.
   - ◦ **Examples:** The 2013 Edward Snowden NSA leak, the 2014 Sony Pictures insider attack, negligent employees causing data breaches.

Common Attack Vectors

1. **Exploiting Software Vulnerabilities:**
   - ◦ Attackers exploit weaknesses in software code to gain unauthorized access, execute arbitrary code, or cause disruptions. Common vulnerabilities include buffer overflows, SQL injection, and cross-site scripting (XSS).

2. **Social Engineering:**
   - ◦ Attackers manipulate individuals into divulging confidential information or performing actions that compromise security. Techniques include phishing, pretexting,

baiting, and tailgating.

3. **Weak Passwords and Credential Theft:**
   - Attackers exploit weak or reused passwords to gain access to accounts. Credential theft techniques include brute force attacks, credential stuffing, and keylogging.

4. **Malware Delivery:**
   - Attackers deliver malware through various means, such as email attachments, malicious websites, USB drives, and drive-by downloads.

5. **Unsecured Networks:**
   - Attackers exploit unsecured networks, such as public Wi-Fi, to intercept data and launch attacks. Techniques include eavesdropping, packet sniffing, and rogue access points.

Motivations Behind Cyber Attacks

1. **Financial Gain:**
   - Many cybercriminals are motivated by the potential for financial profit. This includes activities such as ransomware attacks, credit card fraud, and online scams.

2. **Espionage:**
   - Nation-states and state-sponsored actors often conduct cyber espionage to gather intelligence, steal intellectual property, and gain strategic advantages.

3. **Ideological Beliefs:**
   - Hacktivists conduct attacks to promote their political or social causes. Their activities include website defacements, data leaks, and distributed denial-of-service attacks.

4. **Revenge or Grudge:**
   - Disgruntled employees or individuals may

launch attacks to retaliate against perceived wrongs. These attacks can result in data breaches, sabotage, or reputational damage.

5. **Recreation and Challenge:**
   - Some attackers are motivated by the thrill of the challenge and the desire to demonstrate their technical skills. This category includes many young and amateur hackers.

Case Studies of Notable Cyber Attacks

1. **WannaCry Ransomware Attack (2017):**
   - **Overview:** The WannaCry ransomware attack affected hundreds of thousands of computers across 150 countries, encrypting files and demanding ransom payments in Bitcoin.
   - **Impact:** The attack disrupted businesses, healthcare services, and government operations. It highlighted the importance of patch management and the risks of outdated software.

2. **Equifax Data Breach (2017):**
   - **Overview:** The Equifax data breach exposed the personal information of 147 million individuals, including Social Security numbers, birthdates, and addresses.
   - **Impact:** The breach led to significant financial losses, legal consequences, and damage to Equifax's reputation. It underscored the need for robust security measures and timely vulnerability management.

3. **SolarWinds Supply Chain Attack (2020):**
   - **Overview:** Attackers compromised the SolarWinds Orion software, distributing a malicious update to thousands of customers,

including government agencies and major corporations.

- **Impact:** The attack led to widespread espionage and data breaches, emphasizing the importance of supply chain security and the need for comprehensive threat detection and response.

Emerging Threats and Trends

1. **AI-Powered Attacks:**
   - Attackers are increasingly leveraging artificial intelligence to enhance the sophistication and effectiveness of their attacks. AI can be used to automate tasks, evade detection, and generate convincing phishing campaigns.

2. **Ransomware as a Service (RaaS):**
   - The rise of RaaS platforms allows even novice cybercriminals to launch ransomware attacks. These platforms provide the tools and infrastructure needed to carry out attacks, lowering the barrier to entry.

3. **Deepfakes and Synthetic Media:**
   - Advances in AI have enabled the creation of deepfakes and synthetic media, which can be used to deceive individuals, spread misinformation, and conduct social engineering attacks.

4. **Internet of Things (IoT) Vulnerabilities:**
   - The proliferation of IoT devices introduces new attack vectors and vulnerabilities. Many IoT devices lack robust security features, making them attractive targets for attackers.

5. **Supply Chain Attacks:**
   - Attackers are increasingly targeting supply

chains to compromise organizations indirectly. These attacks exploit vulnerabilities in third-party vendors and service providers to gain access to the target's network.

Conclusion

In this chapter, we have explored the different types of cyber threats, their attack vectors, the motivations behind them, and notable case studies that illustrate their impact. Understanding these threats is crucial for developing effective cybersecurity strategies and defenses. As we move forward in the subsequent chapters,

CHAPTER 3: CYBERSECURITY FRAMEWORKS AND STANDARDS

Overview

Cybersecurity frameworks and standards provide structured approaches and guidelines to help organizations manage and mitigate cybersecurity risks. These frameworks and standards are designed to ensure that organizations implement effective security controls, comply with regulatory requirements, and protect their information assets from cyber threats. In this chapter, we will explore the key cybersecurity frameworks and standards, their importance, and how they can be applied in practice.

Importance of Cybersecurity Frameworks and Standards

1. **Consistency and Standardization:**
   - Cybersecurity frameworks and standards provide a consistent and standardized approach to managing cybersecurity risks. This ensures that all organizations follow best practices and maintain a high level of security.

2. **Regulatory Compliance:**
   - Many industries are subject to regulatory requirements that mandate the

implementation of specific security controls. Cybersecurity frameworks and standards help organizations comply with these regulations and avoid legal and financial penalties.

3. **Risk Management:**
   - By following established frameworks and standards, organizations can systematically identify, assess, and manage cybersecurity risks. This proactive approach helps prevent security incidents and minimizes the impact of potential breaches.

4. **Continuous Improvement:**
   - Cybersecurity is a dynamic field, and threats are constantly evolving. Frameworks and standards encourage continuous improvement by providing mechanisms for regular assessment, monitoring, and updating of security practices.

5. **Stakeholder Confidence:**
   - Adhering to recognized cybersecurity frameworks and standards demonstrates an organization's commitment to security. This builds trust and confidence among customers, partners, and other stakeholders.

Key Cybersecurity Frameworks and Standards

1. **NIST Cybersecurity Framework:**
   - **Overview:** The National Institute of Standards and Technology (NIST) Cybersecurity Framework is a voluntary framework that provides a risk-based approach to managing cybersecurity. It is widely adopted across various industries.
   - **Core Components:**

- **Identify:** Develop an understanding of the organization's cybersecurity risks, assets, and resources.
- **Protect:** Implement appropriate safeguards to protect critical assets and services.
- **Detect:** Establish mechanisms to identify cybersecurity events and incidents.
- **Respond:** Develop and implement plans to respond to detected cybersecurity incidents.
- **Recover:** Develop and implement plans to restore normal operations after a cybersecurity incident.

  ○ **Implementation:** Organizations can use the NIST Cybersecurity Framework to assess their current security posture, identify gaps, and develop a roadmap for improvement.

2. **ISO/IEC 27001:**

   ○ **Overview:** ISO/IEC 27001 is an international standard for information security management systems (ISMS). It provides a systematic approach to managing sensitive company information and ensuring its security.

   ○ **Core Components:**

   - **Context of the Organization:** Understand the internal and external factors that impact information security.
   - **Leadership:** Establish a clear leadership commitment to information security and define roles

and responsibilities.

- **Planning:** Identify information security risks and develop a plan to address them.
- **Support:** Provide the necessary resources, training, and communication to support the ISMS.
- **Operation:** Implement and operate the information security controls.
- **Performance Evaluation:** Monitor, measure, and evaluate the effectiveness of the ISMS.
- **Improvement:** Continuously improve the ISMS based on the results of performance evaluations.

○ **Implementation:** Organizations can achieve ISO/IEC 27001 certification by implementing the standard's requirements and undergoing an independent audit.

3. **CIS Controls:**

○ **Overview:** The Center for Internet Security (CIS) Controls, formerly known as the Critical Security Controls, are a set of best practices for securing IT systems and data. They are designed to help organizations prioritize and implement effective security measures.

○ **Core Components:**

- **Basic Controls:** Fundamental controls that provide essential security measures (e.g., inventory and control of hardware assets, secure configuration of hardware and software).
- **Foundational Controls:** Controls that

build on the basic controls to provide additional layers of security (e.g., continuous vulnerability management, email and web browser protection).

- **Organizational Controls:** Controls that address broader security concerns and organizational practices (e.g., incident response management, penetration testing).

○ **Implementation:** Organizations can use the CIS Controls as a practical guide to enhance their security posture, starting with the most critical controls and progressively implementing more advanced measures.

4. **Industry-Specific Frameworks:**

○ **Overview:** Many industries have specific cybersecurity frameworks and standards tailored to their unique needs and regulatory requirements. These frameworks provide industry-specific guidance on managing cybersecurity risks.

○ **Examples:**

- **Healthcare:** Health Insurance Portability and Accountability Act (HIPAA) Security Rule, Health Information Trust Alliance (HITRUST) Common Security Framework.

- **Finance:** Payment Card Industry Data Security Standard (PCI DSS), Financial Services Sector Coordinating Council (FSSCC) Cybersecurity Profile.

- **Energy:** North American Electric Reliability Corporation Critical

Infrastructure Protection (NERC CIP), National Institute of Standards and Technology (NIST) 800-82 for Industrial Control Systems (ICS).

Applying Cybersecurity Frameworks and Standards

1. **Assessing Current Security Posture:**
   - Organizations should begin by assessing their current security posture using the chosen framework or standard. This involves identifying assets, evaluating existing controls, and assessing vulnerabilities and risks.

2. **Identifying Gaps and Prioritizing Actions:**
   - Based on the assessment, organizations can identify gaps in their security controls and prioritize actions to address these gaps. Prioritization should be based on the potential impact and likelihood of security incidents.

3. **Developing a Roadmap for Improvement:**
   - Organizations should develop a roadmap for improving their security posture. This roadmap should outline specific actions, timelines, and responsibilities for implementing the necessary security controls.

4. **Implementing Security Controls:**
   - Organizations should implement the security controls as outlined in the roadmap. This may involve deploying new technologies, updating policies and procedures, and providing training and awareness programs for employees.

5. **Monitoring and Measuring Effectiveness:**

○ Continuous monitoring and measurement are essential to ensure the effectiveness of the implemented security controls. Organizations should use metrics and key performance indicators (KPIs) to evaluate their security posture and identify areas for improvement.

6. **Continuous Improvement:**

○ Cybersecurity is an ongoing process, and organizations should continuously improve their security practices. This involves regularly reviewing and updating security controls, conducting periodic assessments, and staying informed about emerging threats and best practices.

Conclusion

In this chapter, we have explored the importance of cybersecurity frameworks and standards, key frameworks such as the NIST Cybersecurity Framework, ISO/IEC 27001, and CIS Controls, and industry-specific frameworks. We have also discussed how organizations can apply these frameworks and standards to assess their security posture, identify gaps, prioritize actions, and implement effective security controls. By following established frameworks and standards, organizations can enhance their cybersecurity resilience, comply with regulatory requirements, and protect their information assets from cyber threats. As we move forward in the subsequent chapters, we will delve deeper into specific aspects of cybersecurity, including risk management, network security, endpoint security, and more.

CHAPTER 4: RISK MANAGEMENT AND ASSESSMENT

Overview

Risk management and assessment are critical components of an effective cybersecurity strategy. By identifying, assessing, and mitigating risks, organizations can protect their information assets, ensure business continuity, and comply with regulatory requirements. This chapter explores the principles of cyber risk management, methodologies for risk assessment, and strategies for mitigating risks. We will also discuss the role of risk management frameworks in guiding organizations through the process.

Understanding Cyber Risk

Cyber risk refers to the potential for loss or damage resulting from cyber threats exploiting vulnerabilities in an organization's systems, networks, or data. Effective risk management involves understanding the nature of these risks and implementing measures to mitigate their impact. Key concepts in cyber risk management include:

1. **Asset:** Any resource that has value to an organization and needs protection. Examples include hardware, software, data, intellectual property, and personnel.

2. **Threat:** Any potential event or action that could cause harm to an asset. Examples include malware, phishing attacks, natural disasters, and insider threats.

3. **Vulnerability:** A weakness or flaw in a system that can be exploited by a threat to cause harm. Examples include unpatched software, weak passwords, and misconfigured systems.

4. **Impact:** The potential consequences or damage resulting from a threat exploiting a vulnerability. Impact can be measured in terms of financial loss, reputational damage, legal consequences, and operational disruption.

5. **Likelihood:** The probability that a specific threat will exploit a vulnerability and cause harm. Likelihood can be influenced by factors such as threat actor capabilities, attack vectors, and existing controls.

6. **Risk:** The combination of the likelihood and impact of a threat exploiting a vulnerability. Risk is typically expressed as a function of likelihood and impact (Risk = Likelihood x Impact).

Risk Assessment Methodologies

Risk assessment is the process of identifying, analyzing, and evaluating risks to determine their potential impact and likelihood. There are several methodologies for conducting risk assessments, each with its own strengths and weaknesses. Some common methodologies include:

1. **Qualitative Risk Assessment:**
   - **Description:** A qualitative risk assessment uses subjective judgment to evaluate risks based on their likelihood and impact. Risks are typically categorized as high, medium, or low.
   - **Advantages:** Easy to implement, cost-effective, and provides a quick overview of risks.
   - **Disadvantages:** Subjective and less precise, may lack consistency and repeatability.

- **Steps:**
  - Identify assets, threats, and vulnerabilities.
  - Assess the likelihood and impact of each risk.
  - Categorize risks based on their assessed likelihood and impact.
  - Prioritize risks for mitigation based on their categorization.

2. **Quantitative Risk Assessment:**
   - **Description:** A quantitative risk assessment uses numerical data and statistical methods to evaluate risks. It assigns monetary values to potential losses and calculates the probability of different outcomes.
   - **Advantages:** Provides precise and measurable results, supports cost-benefit analysis.
   - **Disadvantages:** Requires detailed data, time-consuming, and may be complex to implement.
   - **Steps:**
     - Identify assets, threats, and vulnerabilities.
     - Collect data on historical incidents, threat intelligence, and asset values.
     - Calculate the likelihood and impact of each risk using statistical methods.
     - Express risks in monetary terms and prioritize them based on their financial impact.

3. **Semi-Quantitative Risk Assessment:**
   - **Description:** A semi-quantitative risk assessment combines elements of both

qualitative and quantitative approaches. It uses numerical scales to assess likelihood and impact but does not assign specific monetary values.

- **Advantages:** Balances the strengths of qualitative and quantitative methods, provides a more structured and consistent assessment.
- **Disadvantages:** May still involve subjective judgment, requires some data collection.
- **Steps:**
  - Identify assets, threats, and vulnerabilities.
  - Use numerical scales to assess the likelihood and impact of each risk.
  - Calculate risk scores based on the assessed likelihood and impact.
  - Prioritize risks based on their risk scores.

Identifying and Assessing Risks

The risk assessment process typically involves the following steps:

1. **Asset Identification:**
   - Identify and document all assets that need protection. This includes hardware, software, data, intellectual property, and personnel. Create an asset inventory that includes details such as asset value, owner, location, and criticality.

2. **Threat Identification:**
   - Identify and document all potential threats to the identified assets. Consider a wide range of threats, including cyber threats (e.g.,

malware, phishing), physical threats (e.g., natural disasters, theft), and human threats (e.g., insider threats, human error).

3. **Vulnerability Identification:**

   - Identify and document all vulnerabilities that could be exploited by the identified threats. Consider both technical vulnerabilities (e.g., unpatched software, misconfigurations) and non-technical vulnerabilities (e.g., weak policies, lack of training).

4. **Risk Analysis:**

   - Analyze the identified risks to determine their potential impact and likelihood. Use qualitative, quantitative, or semi-quantitative methods to assess each risk. Consider factors such as threat actor capabilities, attack vectors, existing controls, and historical data.

5. **Risk Evaluation:**

   - Evaluate the analyzed risks to determine their significance and prioritize them for mitigation. Consider the organization's risk appetite and tolerance, as well as the potential impact on business objectives.

Risk Mitigation Strategies

Risk mitigation involves implementing measures to reduce the likelihood and impact of identified risks. Common risk mitigation strategies include:

1. **Risk Avoidance:**

   - Eliminate the risk by avoiding the activity or situation that creates the risk. For example, discontinue the use of vulnerable software or processes.

2. **Risk Reduction:**

- Implement controls to reduce the likelihood or impact of the risk. For example, apply security patches, implement multi-factor authentication, or conduct security awareness training.

3. **Risk Transfer:**
   - Transfer the risk to another party, such as through insurance or outsourcing. For example, purchase cyber insurance to cover potential losses from a data breach.

4. **Risk Acceptance:**
   - Accept the risk if it falls within the organization's risk tolerance and does not require additional controls. Document the decision and rationale for accepting the risk.

Risk Management Frameworks

Risk management frameworks provide structured approaches for managing cybersecurity risks. Some widely recognized risk management frameworks include:

1. **NIST Risk Management Framework (RMF):**
   - **Overview:** The NIST RMF provides a structured approach for integrating cybersecurity risk management into the system development lifecycle. It emphasizes continuous monitoring and assessment.
   - **Core Steps:**
     - Categorize: Categorize the system and information based on impact levels.
     - Select: Select appropriate security controls.
     - Implement: Implement the selected security controls.
     - Assess: Assess the effectiveness of the

security controls.

- Authorize: Authorize the system for operation based on risk acceptance.
- Monitor: Continuously monitor the system and security controls.

2. **ISO/IEC 27005:**

   ◦ **Overview:** ISO/IEC 27005 provides guidelines for information security risk management within the context of an information security management system (ISMS) as specified in ISO/IEC 27001.

   ◦ **Core Steps:**

   - Context Establishment: Define the context, scope, and criteria for risk management.
   - Risk Assessment: Identify, analyze, and evaluate risks.
   - Risk Treatment: Select and implement risk treatment options.
   - Risk Communication: Communicate risk information to relevant stakeholders.
   - Risk Monitoring and Review: Monitor and review risks and the effectiveness of risk treatment.

3. **OCTAVE (Operationally Critical Threat, Asset, and Vulnerability Evaluation):**

   ◦ **Overview:** OCTAVE is a risk assessment methodology developed by Carnegie Mellon University. It focuses on assessing organizational risks and developing mitigation strategies.

   ◦ **Core Phases:**

- Phase 1: Build Asset-Based Threat Profiles.
- Phase 2: Identify Infrastructure Vulnerabilities.
- Phase 3: Develop Security Strategy and Plan.

Conclusion

In this chapter, we have explored the principles of cyber risk management, methodologies for risk assessment, and strategies for mitigating risks. We have also discussed the role of risk management frameworks in guiding organizations through the risk management process. By understanding and implementing effective risk management practices, organizations can protect their information assets, ensure business continuity, and comply with regulatory requirements. As we move forward in the subsequent chapters, we will delve deeper into specific aspects of cybersecurity, including security policies, network security, endpoint security, and more.

CHAPTER 5: SECURITY POLICIES AND GOVERNANCE

Overview

Security policies and governance are fundamental components of an effective cybersecurity strategy. Security policies provide a structured approach to managing and protecting information assets, while governance ensures that security measures are implemented, monitored, and continuously improved. This chapter explores the importance of security policies, the process of developing and implementing effective policies, governance models, compliance with regulatory requirements, and best practices for policy enforcement.

Importance of Security Policies

Security policies serve as the foundation for an organization's cybersecurity framework. They establish the rules and guidelines that govern how information assets are protected and how employees, contractors, and third parties should behave in relation to those assets. Key reasons for having security policies include:

1. **Risk Mitigation:**
   - Security policies help identify and address potential risks and vulnerabilities, reducing the likelihood of security incidents and breaches.

2. **Compliance:**
   - Many industries are subject to regulatory requirements that mandate specific security measures. Security policies ensure that organizations comply with these regulations and avoid legal and financial penalties.

3. **Consistency:**
   - Policies provide a consistent approach to security across the organization, ensuring that all employees and stakeholders understand their responsibilities and adhere to the same standards.

4. **Accountability:**
   - Security policies establish clear roles and responsibilities for managing and protecting information assets, holding individuals accountable for their actions.

5. **Incident Response:**
   - Policies outline the procedures for detecting, responding to, and recovering from security incidents, ensuring a coordinated and effective response.

Developing Effective Security Policies

Developing effective security policies involves several key steps:

1. **Identify Security Objectives:**
   - Define the security objectives that the policies are intended to achieve. These objectives should align with the organization's overall business goals and risk management strategy.

2. **Assess Risks and Requirements:**
   - Conduct a risk assessment to identify potential threats, vulnerabilities, and impacts. Consider regulatory requirements,

industry standards, and best practices when determining the necessary security controls.

3. **Engage Stakeholders:**
   - Involve key stakeholders in the policy development process, including senior management, IT staff, legal and compliance teams, and business unit leaders. Their input and support are crucial for the successful implementation of policies.

4. **Draft Policies:**
   - Write clear, concise, and comprehensive policies that address identified risks and requirements. Policies should be tailored to the organization's specific needs and context.

5. **Review and Approve:**
   - Review the drafted policies with relevant stakeholders to ensure accuracy and completeness. Obtain formal approval from senior management before finalizing the policies.

6. **Communicate and Train:**
   - Communicate the approved policies to all employees and stakeholders. Provide training and awareness programs to ensure that everyone understands the policies and their responsibilities.

7. **Monitor and Update:**
   - Continuously monitor the effectiveness of the policies and update them as needed to address emerging threats, changes in regulations, and evolving business needs.

Key Components of Security Policies

Security policies should cover a wide range of topics to address various aspects of cybersecurity. Some key components of security policies include:

1. **Acceptable Use Policy (AUP):**
   - Defines the acceptable and unacceptable use of organizational resources, including computers, networks, and data. The AUP outlines user responsibilities and prohibited activities.

2. **Access Control Policy:**
   - Specifies the procedures for granting, modifying, and revoking access to information systems and data. The policy should include guidelines for authentication, authorization, and account management.

3. **Data Protection Policy:**
   - Outlines the measures for protecting sensitive and confidential data, including data classification, encryption, data retention, and data disposal. The policy should also address data privacy requirements.

4. **Incident Response Policy:**
   - Defines the procedures for detecting, reporting, and responding to security incidents. The policy should include guidelines for incident investigation, communication, and recovery.

5. **Network Security Policy:**
   - Specifies the measures for securing the organization's network infrastructure, including firewalls, intrusion detection and prevention systems, virtual private networks (VPNs), and network segmentation.

6. **Password Policy:**

- Establishes the requirements for creating, managing, and protecting passwords. The policy should include guidelines for password complexity, expiration, and storage.

7. **Mobile Device Policy:**
   - Defines the rules for using and securing mobile devices, including smartphones, tablets, and laptops. The policy should address device management, encryption, and remote access.

8. **Third-Party Access Policy:**
   - Outlines the procedures for granting and managing access to organizational resources by third parties, such as vendors, contractors, and partners. The policy should include guidelines for third-party risk assessment and monitoring.

Governance Models and Best Practices

Effective cybersecurity governance ensures that security policies are implemented, monitored, and continuously improved. Key components of a robust governance model include:

1. **Security Leadership:**
   - Establish a dedicated security leadership team, such as a Chief Information Security Officer (CISO) and security managers, to oversee the development and implementation of security policies and practices.

2. **Security Committees:**
   - Form security committees or working groups that include representatives from various departments, such as IT, legal, compliance, HR, and business units. These committees

should regularly review and discuss security issues and initiatives.

3. **Security Frameworks:**
   - Adopt and implement recognized security frameworks and standards, such as ISO/IEC 27001, NIST Cybersecurity Framework, and CIS Controls, to guide the organization's security practices.

4. **Regular Assessments:**
   - Conduct regular security assessments, audits, and penetration tests to evaluate the effectiveness of security controls and identify areas for improvement.

5. **Performance Metrics:**
   - Establish key performance indicators (KPIs) and metrics to measure the effectiveness of security policies and practices. Use these metrics to track progress and inform decision-making.

6. **Continuous Improvement:**
   - Foster a culture of continuous improvement by encouraging feedback, learning from incidents, and staying informed about emerging threats and best practices.

Compliance and Regulatory Requirements

Compliance with regulatory requirements is a critical aspect of cybersecurity governance. Organizations must ensure that their security policies and practices align with relevant laws, regulations, and industry standards. Key regulatory requirements include:

1. **General Data Protection Regulation (GDPR):**
   - GDPR is a comprehensive data protection regulation that applies to organizations

processing personal data of individuals in the European Union. It mandates strict requirements for data protection, privacy, and breach notification.

2. **Health Insurance Portability and Accountability Act (HIPAA):**

   ◦ HIPAA is a U.S. regulation that sets standards for the protection of health information. It requires healthcare organizations to implement measures to ensure the confidentiality, integrity, and availability of patient data.

3. **Payment Card Industry Data Security Standard (PCI DSS):**

   ◦ PCI DSS is a set of security standards designed to protect payment card information. It applies to organizations that handle cardholder data and mandates specific security controls and practices.

4. **Sarbanes-Oxley Act (SOX):**

   ◦ SOX is a U.S. regulation that requires publicly traded companies to implement controls and procedures for financial reporting. It includes requirements for information security and internal controls.

5. **Gramm-Leach-Bliley Act (GLBA):**

   ◦ GLBA is a U.S. regulation that requires financial institutions to protect customer information. It mandates the development and implementation of security policies and practices.

Policy Implementation and Enforcement

Implementing and enforcing security policies is essential for ensuring their effectiveness. Key steps for policy implementation and enforcement include:

1. **Communication:**
   - Clearly communicate the policies to all employees, contractors, and third parties. Use various channels, such as email, intranet, and training sessions, to ensure everyone is aware of the policies.

2. **Training and Awareness:**
   - Provide regular training and awareness programs to educate employees about security policies, their responsibilities, and best practices. Use interactive and engaging methods to reinforce key messages.

3. **Monitoring and Auditing:**
   - Monitor compliance with security policies through regular audits, assessments, and automated tools. Identify and address any deviations or violations promptly.

4. **Enforcement:**
   - Enforce security policies consistently and fairly. Use a combination of disciplinary actions, incentives, and rewards to encourage compliance and deter violations.

5. **Review and Update:**
   - Regularly review and update security policies to ensure they remain relevant and effective. Consider feedback from employees, lessons learned from incidents, and changes in the threat landscape.

Conclusion

In this chapter, we have explored the importance of security policies and governance in an effective cybersecurity strategy. We discussed the process of developing and implementing effective policies, key components of security policies, governance models, compliance with regulatory requirements, and best practices for policy enforcement. By establishing and enforcing robust security policies and governance, organizations can protect their information assets, ensure compliance, and mitigate cybersecurity risks. As we move forward in the subsequent chapters, we will delve deeper into specific aspects of cybersecurity, including network security, endpoint security, identity and access management, and more.

CHAPTER 6:
NETWORK SECURITY

Overview

Network security is a critical component of an organization's cybersecurity strategy. It involves implementing measures and controls to protect the integrity, confidentiality, and availability of network infrastructure and data. With the increasing reliance on networked systems and the growing sophistication of cyber threats, securing networks has become more important than ever. This chapter explores the fundamentals of network security, key technologies and protocols, common threats and vulnerabilities, and best practices for securing networks.

Fundamentals of Network Security

Network security encompasses a range of practices and technologies designed to protect networks and their associated data. Key principles of network security include:

1. **Confidentiality:**
   - Ensuring that sensitive information is accessible only to authorized users and systems. Confidentiality is achieved through encryption, access controls, and secure communication protocols.

2. **Integrity:**
   - Ensuring that data is accurate, complete, and has not been tampered with. Integrity is maintained through hashing, digital signatures, and integrity checks.

3. **Availability:**
   - Ensuring that network resources and services are available to authorized users when needed. Availability is achieved through redundancy, fault tolerance, and robust network design.

4. **Authentication:**
   - Verifying the identity of users and devices before granting access to network resources. Authentication is implemented through passwords, biometrics, multi-factor authentication, and digital certificates.

5. **Authorization:**
   - Granting access to network resources based on predefined policies and user roles. Authorization is enforced through access control lists (ACLs) and role-based access control (RBAC).

6. **Accounting:**
   - Tracking and recording user activities on the network for auditing and accountability purposes. Accounting is achieved through logging, monitoring, and auditing mechanisms.

Key Network Security Technologies and Protocols

1. **Firewalls:**
   - **Description:** Firewalls are network security devices that monitor and control incoming and outgoing network traffic based on predefined security rules. They act as a barrier between trusted and untrusted networks.
   - **Types:**
     - **Packet-Filtering Firewalls:** Inspect

packets and allow or block them based on source and destination IP addresses, ports, and protocols.

- **Stateful Inspection Firewalls:** Monitor the state of active connections and make decisions based on the context of the traffic.
- **Next-Generation Firewalls (NGFWs):** Incorporate advanced features such as application awareness, intrusion prevention, and deep packet inspection.

2. **Intrusion Detection and Prevention Systems (IDPS):**
   - **Description:** IDPS are network security devices that detect and respond to malicious activities and policy violations. They can be deployed as either intrusion detection systems (IDS) or intrusion prevention systems (IPS).
   - **Types:**
     - **Network-Based IDPS (NIDPS):** Monitor network traffic for suspicious activities and generate alerts or take action.
     - **Host-Based IDPS (HIDPS):** Monitor activities on individual hosts or devices for signs of compromise.

3. **Virtual Private Networks (VPNs):**
   - **Description:** VPNs provide secure communication over public networks by encrypting data and creating a private tunnel between endpoints. They are commonly used for remote access and secure communication between sites.

○ **Types:**

- **Remote Access VPNs:** Allow individual users to securely connect to a private network from a remote location.
- **Site-to-Site VPNs:** Connect entire networks at different locations, enabling secure communication between them.

4. **Network Segmentation:**

○ **Description:** Network segmentation involves dividing a network into smaller, isolated segments to limit the spread of threats and improve security. Segmentation is achieved through VLANs, subnets, and access control policies.

○ **Benefits:** Enhanced security, improved performance, and simplified management.

5. **Secure Communication Protocols:**

○ **Description:** Secure communication protocols ensure the confidentiality, integrity, and authenticity of data transmitted over networks.

○ **Examples:**

- **TLS/SSL:** Transport Layer Security (TLS) and Secure Sockets Layer (SSL) are protocols that provide secure communication over the internet.
- **IPSec:** Internet Protocol Security (IPSec) is a suite of protocols that secure IP communications by authenticating and encrypting each IP packet.

- **SSH:** Secure Shell (SSH) is a protocol that provides secure remote access and command execution over an encrypted connection.

Common Network Security Threats and Vulnerabilities

1. **Malware:**
   - Malware can spread through networks, compromising systems and data. Common network-based malware threats include worms, ransomware, and botnets.

2. **Phishing:**
   - Phishing attacks often target network credentials, leading to unauthorized access to network resources. Spear-phishing and whaling attacks can compromise high-value accounts.

3. **Man-in-the-Middle (MitM) Attacks:**
   - MitM attacks involve intercepting and manipulating communication between parties. Attackers can eavesdrop, alter data, and steal sensitive information.

4. **Denial-of-Service (DoS) Attacks:**
   - DoS attacks overwhelm network resources, rendering them unavailable to users. DDoS attacks amplify this effect by using multiple compromised systems.

5. **Unpatched Vulnerabilities:**
   - Unpatched software and firmware can expose networks to exploitation. Attackers can exploit known vulnerabilities to gain unauthorized access or cause disruptions.

6. **Weak Authentication and Authorization:**
   - Weak passwords, lack of multi-factor

authentication, and improper access controls can lead to unauthorized access to network resources.

7. **Insider Threats:**
   ◦ Insider threats, whether malicious or accidental, can compromise network security. Employees and contractors with access to sensitive data can pose significant risks.

Best Practices for Securing Networks

1. **Implement Strong Access Controls:**
   ◦ Use strong authentication mechanisms, such as multi-factor authentication, to verify the identity of users and devices. Implement role-based access control (RBAC) to limit access based on user roles and responsibilities.

2. **Regularly Update and Patch Systems:**
   ◦ Keep all software, firmware, and hardware up to date with the latest security patches. Regularly scan for vulnerabilities and apply patches promptly.

3. **Use Firewalls and IDPS:**
   ◦ Deploy firewalls to monitor and control network traffic. Use intrusion detection and prevention systems (IDPS) to detect and respond to suspicious activities.

4. **Encrypt Data in Transit:**
   ◦ Use secure communication protocols, such as TLS/SSL and IPSec, to encrypt data transmitted over networks. Ensure that sensitive information is protected during transmission.

5. **Implement Network Segmentation:**
   ◦ Divide the network into smaller segments

to limit the spread of threats and contain potential breaches. Use VLANs and access control policies to enforce segmentation.

6. **Monitor and Log Network Activity:**
   ◦ Continuously monitor network traffic and log activities to detect and investigate suspicious behavior. Use security information and event management (SIEM) tools to analyze and correlate log data.

7. **Conduct Regular Security Assessments:**
   ◦ Perform regular security assessments, including vulnerability scans, penetration tests, and audits, to identify and address potential weaknesses.

8. **Educate and Train Employees:**
   ◦ Provide regular cybersecurity training and awareness programs for employees to educate them about network security best practices, social engineering attacks, and their role in protecting the network.

Conclusion

In this chapter, we have explored the fundamentals of network security, key technologies and protocols, common threats and vulnerabilities, and best practices for securing networks. Network security is a critical component of an organization's cybersecurity strategy, and implementing effective measures is essential for protecting network infrastructure and data. As we move forward in the subsequent chapters, we will delve deeper into specific aspects of cybersecurity, including endpoint security, identity and access management, data protection, and more. By understanding and applying the principles and best practices of network security, organizations can enhance their resilience against cyber threats and safeguard their information assets.

CHAPTER 7:
ENDPOINT SECURITY

Overview

Endpoint security is a critical aspect of an organization's overall cybersecurity strategy. Endpoints, such as desktops, laptops, mobile devices, and IoT devices, are often the primary targets for cyberattacks. Protecting these endpoints is essential to prevent unauthorized access, data breaches, and the spread of malware. This chapter explores the fundamentals of endpoint security, key technologies and solutions, common threats, and best practices for securing endpoints.

Fundamentals of Endpoint Security

Endpoint security involves implementing measures and controls to protect endpoint devices from cyber threats. Key principles of endpoint security include:

1. **Confidentiality:**
   - Ensuring that sensitive data on endpoints is accessible only to authorized users. Confidentiality is maintained through encryption, access controls, and secure storage.

2. **Integrity:**
   - Ensuring that data on endpoints is accurate, complete, and has not been tampered with. Integrity is maintained through hashing, digital signatures, and integrity checks.

3. **Availability:**
    - Ensuring that endpoint devices and their data are available to authorized users when needed. Availability is achieved through regular maintenance, updates, and backups.

4. **Authentication:**
    - Verifying the identity of users and devices before granting access to endpoint resources. Authentication is implemented through passwords, biometrics, multi-factor authentication, and digital certificates.

5. **Authorization:**
    - Granting access to endpoint resources based on predefined policies and user roles. Authorization is enforced through access control lists (ACLs) and role-based access control (RBAC).

Key Endpoint Security Technologies and Solutions

1. **Endpoint Protection Platforms (EPP):**
    - **Description:** EPP solutions provide comprehensive security for endpoint devices by integrating various security functions, such as antivirus, anti-malware, firewall, and intrusion prevention.
    - **Examples:** Symantec Endpoint Protection, McAfee Endpoint Security, Trend Micro Apex One.

2. **Endpoint Detection and Response (EDR):**
    - **Description:** EDR solutions focus on detecting and responding to advanced threats on endpoint devices. They provide continuous monitoring, threat detection, and incident response capabilities.

- **Examples:** CrowdStrike Falcon, Carbon Black Response, SentinelOne.

3. **Antivirus and Anti-Malware:**

- **Description:** Antivirus and anti-malware software scan endpoint devices for malicious software and remove or quarantine any detected threats. They use signature-based detection, heuristics, and behavioral analysis.
- **Examples:** Norton Antivirus, Bitdefender, Kaspersky Anti-Virus.

4. **Device Management and Control:**

- **Description:** Device management solutions help organizations manage and secure endpoint devices, including desktops, laptops, mobile devices, and IoT devices. They provide features such as device inventory, remote management, and policy enforcement.
- **Examples:** Microsoft Intune, VMware Workspace ONE, IBM MaaS360.

5. **Encryption:**

- **Description:** Encryption solutions protect data on endpoint devices by converting it into unreadable code that can only be decrypted with the correct key. This ensures the confidentiality of sensitive data, even if the device is lost or stolen.
- **Examples:** BitLocker, VeraCrypt, Symantec Encryption.

6. **Mobile Device Management (MDM):**

- **Description:** MDM solutions focus on securing and managing mobile devices, such as smartphones and tablets. They provide features such as device enrollment, remote wipe, app management, and security policy enforcement.

- **Examples:** MobileIron, AirWatch, Jamf Pro.

Common Endpoint Security Threats

1. **Malware:**
   - Malware, such as viruses, worms, trojans, ransomware, and spyware, can infect endpoint devices and cause significant damage. Malware can steal data, encrypt files, disrupt operations, and provide unauthorized access to attackers.

2. **Phishing:**
   - Phishing attacks often target endpoint users to trick them into revealing sensitive information, such as login credentials, financial information, or personal data. Phishing attacks can be delivered via email, SMS, social media, or malicious websites.

3. **Ransomware:**
   - Ransomware is a type of malware that encrypts files on endpoint devices and demands payment for the decryption key. Ransomware attacks can result in data loss, downtime, and financial losses.

4. **Unauthorized Access:**
   - Endpoint devices can be compromised by unauthorized users who gain access through weak passwords, stolen credentials, or unpatched vulnerabilities. Unauthorized access can lead to data breaches and the spread of malware.

5. **Insider Threats:**
   - Insider threats involve employees,

contractors, or third parties who misuse their access privileges to compromise endpoint security. Insider threats can be intentional or accidental and can result in data theft, sabotage, or policy violations.

Best Practices for Securing Endpoints

1. **Implement Strong Authentication:**
   - Use strong authentication mechanisms, such as multi-factor authentication (MFA), to verify the identity of users and devices. Implement password policies that require complex and unique passwords.

2. **Keep Software and Firmware Updated:**
   - Regularly update and patch endpoint devices to address known vulnerabilities. Enable automatic updates to ensure that devices receive the latest security patches.

3. **Deploy Endpoint Protection Solutions:**
   - Use endpoint protection platforms (EPP) and endpoint detection and response (EDR) solutions to protect endpoint devices from malware, ransomware, and advanced threats. Regularly scan devices for threats and respond promptly to any detected incidents.

4. **Encrypt Sensitive Data:**
   - Use encryption to protect sensitive data on endpoint devices. Encrypt data at rest (stored data) and data in transit (data being transmitted) to ensure confidentiality.

5. **Enable Device Management and Control:**
   - Use device management solutions to manage and secure endpoint devices. Implement security policies, monitor device compliance,

and remotely manage devices.

6. **Educate and Train Users:**
   - Provide regular cybersecurity training and awareness programs for endpoint users. Educate users about common threats, such as phishing and malware, and best practices for protecting endpoint devices.

7. **Implement Network Segmentation:**
   - Use network segmentation to isolate endpoint devices and limit the spread of threats. Create separate network segments for different types of devices and apply access controls to restrict communication between segments.

8. **Regularly Back Up Data:**
   - Regularly back up data on endpoint devices to protect against data loss due to ransomware, hardware failure, or other incidents. Store backups in secure, offsite locations and test backup and recovery procedures.

9. **Monitor and Log Endpoint Activity:**
   - Continuously monitor and log activities on endpoint devices to detect and investigate suspicious behavior. Use security information and event management (SIEM) tools to analyze and correlate log data.

10. **Implement Security Policies and Governance:**
    - Develop and enforce security policies that govern the use and protection of endpoint devices. Regularly review and update policies to address emerging threats and changes in the threat landscape.

Conclusion

In this chapter, we have explored the fundamentals of endpoint security, key technologies and solutions, common threats, and best practices for securing endpoints. Endpoint security is a critical aspect of an organization's overall cybersecurity strategy, and implementing effective measures is essential for protecting endpoint devices and data. As we move forward in the subsequent chapters, we will delve deeper into specific aspects of cybersecurity, including identity and access management, data protection, cloud security, and more. By understanding and applying the principles and best practices of endpoint security, organizations can enhance their resilience against cyber threats and safeguard their information assets.

CHAPTER 8: IDENTITY AND ACCESS MANAGEMENT (IAM)

Overview

Identity and Access Management (IAM) is a critical component of an organization's cybersecurity strategy. IAM involves the processes and technologies used to manage and control access to information systems and data based on the identities of users and devices. Effective IAM ensures that only authorized users have access to the resources they need, while protecting sensitive information from unauthorized access. This chapter explores the fundamentals of IAM, key components and technologies, common challenges, and best practices for implementing and managing IAM.

Fundamentals of Identity and Access Management

IAM encompasses a wide range of processes and technologies designed to manage digital identities and control access to resources. Key principles of IAM include:

1. **Identification:**
   - The process of identifying users and devices based on unique identifiers, such as usernames, email addresses, or device IDs.

2. **Authentication:**
   - The process of verifying the identity of users and devices before granting

access to resources. Authentication methods include passwords, biometrics, multi-factor authentication (MFA), and digital certificates.

3. **Authorization:**
   - The process of granting or denying access to resources based on the authenticated identity and predefined access policies. Authorization is enforced through access control lists (ACLs), role-based access control (RBAC), and attribute-based access control (ABAC).

4. **Accounting (Auditing):**
   - The process of tracking and recording user activities on information systems for auditing and accountability purposes. This includes logging access attempts, changes to permissions, and other relevant actions.

Key Components and Technologies of IAM

1. **User Identity Management:**
   - **Description:** User identity management involves creating, managing, and maintaining user identities and attributes throughout their lifecycle. This includes user provisioning, de-provisioning, and self-service account management.
   - **Technologies:** Identity governance and administration (IGA) solutions, directory services (e.g., Active Directory), identity synchronization tools.

2. **Authentication:**
   - **Description:** Authentication ensures that users and devices are who they claim to be before granting access to resources. Strong authentication methods enhance security by reducing the risk of unauthorized access.

- **Technologies:** Passwords, multi-factor authentication (MFA), biometrics, single sign-on (SSO), digital certificates, hardware tokens.

3. **Authorization:**

   - **Description:** Authorization controls determine what resources users and devices can access based on their identity and roles. Effective authorization mechanisms enforce the principle of least privilege, ensuring that users have only the access they need.

   - **Technologies:** Role-based access control (RBAC), attribute-based access control (ABAC), access control lists (ACLs), policy-based access control.

4. **Access Management:**

   - **Description:** Access management involves managing and controlling access to applications, systems, and data based on predefined policies. This includes access requests, approvals, and enforcement of access policies.

   - **Technologies:** Access management solutions (e.g., Okta, Ping Identity), web access management (WAM), federated identity management.

5. **Identity Federation:**

   - **Description:** Identity federation allows users to use a single set of credentials to access multiple applications or systems across different domains. This enhances user convenience and security by reducing the need for multiple usernames and passwords.

   - **Technologies:** Security Assertion Markup Language (SAML), OpenID Connect, OAuth, federated identity providers.

6. **Privileged Access Management (PAM):**
   - **Description:** PAM involves managing and controlling access to privileged accounts and resources. Privileged accounts have elevated access rights and are often targeted by attackers.
   - **Technologies:** Privileged access management solutions (e.g., CyberArk, BeyondTrust), password vaults, session monitoring, just-in-time access.

Common Challenges in IAM

1. **Complexity of User Management:**
   - Managing user identities and access permissions can be complex, especially in large organizations with diverse user populations and multiple applications. This complexity can lead to errors and security vulnerabilities.

2. **Weak Authentication Practices:**
   - Weak passwords, lack of multi-factor authentication (MFA), and inadequate authentication mechanisms increase the risk of unauthorized access. Organizations must adopt stronger authentication practices to enhance security.

3. **Access Creep:**
   - Over time, users may accumulate access permissions that exceed their current needs. This can result in excessive access rights and increased security risks. Regular reviews and access recertification are essential to address access creep.

4. **Managing Privileged Accounts:**

   ◦ Privileged accounts with elevated access rights pose significant security risks if not properly managed. Organizations must implement robust PAM practices to protect these accounts from misuse and compromise.

5. **Integration with Legacy Systems:**

   ◦ Integrating IAM solutions with legacy systems and applications can be challenging. Organizations must ensure compatibility and interoperability to achieve a seamless IAM implementation.

6. **Compliance and Regulatory Requirements:**

   ◦ Organizations must comply with various regulations and standards related to identity and access management. Achieving and maintaining compliance requires continuous monitoring, auditing, and reporting.

Best Practices for Implementing and Managing IAM

1. **Implement Strong Authentication:**

   ◦ Use strong authentication methods, such as multi-factor authentication (MFA), to enhance security. Implement password policies that require complex and unique passwords.

2. **Adopt Role-Based Access Control (RBAC):**

   ◦ Implement role-based access control (RBAC) to grant access based on predefined roles and responsibilities. Regularly review and update roles to ensure they align with current business needs.

3. **Conduct Regular Access Reviews:**

   ◦ Perform regular access reviews and

recertification to ensure that users have only the access they need. Identify and remove excessive access permissions to reduce security risks.

4. **Implement Privileged Access Management (PAM):**
   ◦ Use PAM solutions to manage and control access to privileged accounts. Implement practices such as password vaulting, session monitoring, and just-in-time access to protect privileged accounts.

5. **Enable Single Sign-On (SSO):**
   ◦ Implement single sign-on (SSO) to provide a seamless and secure authentication experience for users. SSO reduces the need for multiple passwords and enhances user convenience.

6. **Ensure Identity Federation:**
   ◦ Use identity federation technologies to enable users to access multiple applications and systems with a single set of credentials. This simplifies user management and enhances security.

7. **Enforce Least Privilege:**
   ◦ Apply the principle of least privilege to ensure that users have only the access they need to perform their tasks. Regularly review and adjust access permissions to align with job requirements.

8. **Monitor and Log Access Activities:**
   ◦ Continuously monitor and log access activities to detect and investigate suspicious behavior. Use security information and event management (SIEM) tools to analyze and correlate access logs.

9. **Provide User Training and Awareness:**
   ○ Educate users about the importance of IAM and best practices for managing their identities and access permissions. Provide regular training and awareness programs to reinforce key concepts.

10. **Maintain Compliance with Regulations:**
    ○ Ensure that IAM practices comply with relevant regulations and standards. Conduct regular audits and assessments to identify and address compliance gaps.

Conclusion

In this chapter, we have explored the fundamentals of Identity and Access Management (IAM), key components and technologies, common challenges, and best practices for implementing and managing IAM. Effective IAM is essential for protecting information assets, ensuring secure access to resources, and maintaining compliance with regulatory requirements. As we move forward in the subsequent chapters, we will delve deeper into specific aspects of cybersecurity, including data protection, cloud security, application security, and more. By understanding and applying the principles and best practices of IAM, organizations can enhance their resilience against cyber threats and safeguard their digital identities and resources.

CHAPTER 9: DATA PROTECTION AND ENCRYPTION

Overview

Data protection and encryption are crucial aspects of an organization's cybersecurity strategy. Protecting sensitive data from unauthorized access, theft, and loss is essential to ensure confidentiality, integrity, and compliance with regulatory requirements. This chapter explores the fundamentals of data protection, key encryption techniques and algorithms, data loss prevention (DLP) solutions, and best practices for secure data storage and transmission.

Importance of Data Protection

Data protection encompasses a range of measures and practices designed to safeguard sensitive information from unauthorized access and misuse. Key reasons for prioritizing data protection include:

1. **Confidentiality:**
   - Ensuring that sensitive data is accessible only to authorized individuals and systems. This prevents unauthorized disclosure of personal, financial, and proprietary information.

2. **Integrity:**
   - Ensuring that data remains accurate, complete, and unaltered. Data integrity

prevents unauthorized modifications, tampering, and data corruption.

3. **Compliance:**
   - Many industries are subject to regulatory requirements that mandate specific data protection measures. Compliance with these regulations is essential to avoid legal and financial penalties.

4. **Reputation:**
   - Data breaches and unauthorized disclosures can damage an organization's reputation and erode trust with customers, partners, and stakeholders. Robust data protection measures help maintain a positive reputation.

5. **Business Continuity:**
   - Protecting data is essential for ensuring business continuity in the event of cyberattacks, natural disasters, or other disruptions. Effective data protection measures support recovery and resilience.

Data Classification and Handling

Data classification is the process of categorizing data based on its sensitivity and importance. Proper data classification enables organizations to apply appropriate protection measures based on the classification level. Key steps in data classification and handling include:

1. **Identify Data Types:**
   - Identify and document the types of data used and stored by the organization. Examples include personal data, financial data, intellectual property, and operational data.

2. **Define Classification Levels:**
   - Establish classification levels based on

the sensitivity and criticality of the data. Common classification levels include public, internal, confidential, and highly confidential.

3. **Classify Data:**
    ◦ Assign classification levels to data based on predefined criteria. This involves reviewing data content, context, and regulatory requirements.

4. **Label and Tag Data:**
    ◦ Label and tag data with its classification level to ensure proper handling and protection. This can be done manually or through automated tools.

5. **Implement Protection Measures:**
    ◦ Apply protection measures based on the classification level. Highly confidential data may require encryption, access controls, and monitoring, while public data may have fewer restrictions.

6. **Regularly Review and Update Classifications:**
    ◦ Regularly review and update data classifications to ensure they remain accurate and relevant. Changes in business processes, regulations, and data usage may necessitate reclassification.

Encryption Techniques and Algorithms

Encryption is the process of converting plaintext data into unreadable ciphertext using a cryptographic algorithm and key. Encryption ensures that sensitive data remains confidential, even if it is intercepted or accessed by unauthorized individuals. Key encryption techniques and algorithms include:

1. **Symmetric Encryption:**

- **Description:** Symmetric encryption uses the same key for both encryption and decryption. It is efficient and suitable for encrypting large amounts of data.
- **Algorithms:** Advanced Encryption Standard (AES), Data Encryption Standard (DES), Triple DES (3DES).

2. **Asymmetric Encryption:**

- **Description:** Asymmetric encryption uses a pair of keys – a public key for encryption and a private key for decryption. It provides secure key exchange and is commonly used for digital signatures and secure communication.
- **Algorithms:** RSA (Rivest-Shamir-Adleman), Elliptic Curve Cryptography (ECC), Diffie-Hellman (DH).

3. **Hash Functions:**

- **Description:** Hash functions generate a fixed-size hash value from input data. Hash functions are used for data integrity and authentication, as they detect any changes to the original data.
- **Algorithms:** SHA-2 (Secure Hash Algorithm 2), SHA-3 (Secure Hash Algorithm 3), MD5 (Message Digest Algorithm 5).

4. **Digital Signatures:**

- **Description:** Digital signatures use asymmetric encryption to verify the authenticity and integrity of digital messages and documents. They provide non-repudiation, ensuring that the sender cannot deny sending the message.
- **Algorithms:** RSA, DSA (Digital Signature

Algorithm), ECDSA (Elliptic Curve Digital Signature Algorithm).

5. **Key Management:**

- **Description:** Key management involves generating, distributing, storing, and protecting cryptographic keys. Effective key management is essential for maintaining the security of encryption systems.

- **Technologies:** Hardware Security Modules (HSMs), Key Management Services (KMS), Public Key Infrastructure (PKI).

Data Loss Prevention (DLP) Solutions

Data Loss Prevention (DLP) solutions help organizations protect sensitive data from unauthorized access, loss, and leakage. DLP solutions monitor, detect, and block unauthorized data transfers and enforce data protection policies. Key components of DLP solutions include:

1. **Data Discovery and Classification:**

- **Description:** DLP solutions identify and classify sensitive data across the organization. This includes structured data (e.g., databases) and unstructured data (e.g., emails, documents).

2. **Policy Definition and Enforcement:**

- **Description:** DLP solutions allow organizations to define data protection policies based on data classification levels, regulatory requirements, and business needs. Policies specify actions to be taken when unauthorized data transfers are detected.

3. **Monitoring and Detection:**

- **Description:** DLP solutions continuously monitor data in use (e.g., endpoint activities), data in motion (e.g., network traffic), and data at rest (e.g., storage systems). They detect and alert on policy violations and suspicious activities.

4. **Incident Response and Reporting:**
   ◦ **Description:** DLP solutions provide incident response capabilities to investigate and respond to data breaches and policy violations. They generate reports and logs for auditing and compliance purposes.

5. **Integration with Other Security Solutions:**
   ◦ **Description:** DLP solutions integrate with other security technologies, such as encryption, access controls, and SIEM (Security Information and Event Management), to provide comprehensive data protection.

Best Practices for Secure Data Storage and Transmission

1. **Encrypt Sensitive Data:**
   ◦ Encrypt sensitive data at rest and in transit to ensure confidentiality. Use strong encryption algorithms, such as AES for symmetric encryption and RSA for asymmetric encryption.

2. **Implement Access Controls:**
   ◦ Use access controls to restrict access to sensitive data based on the principle of least privilege. Implement role-based access control (RBAC) and attribute-based access control (ABAC) to enforce access policies.

3. **Use Secure Communication Protocols:**
   ◦ Use secure communication protocols, such as TLS/SSL, IPSec, and SSH, to protect

data transmitted over networks. Ensure that endpoints and servers are configured to use secure protocols.

4. **Regularly Back Up Data:**
   - Regularly back up data to protect against data loss due to cyberattacks, hardware failures, or other incidents. Store backups in secure, offsite locations and test backup and recovery procedures.

5. **Monitor and Log Data Access:**
   - Continuously monitor and log data access activities to detect and investigate suspicious behavior. Use SIEM tools to analyze and correlate log data.

6. **Implement Data Masking and Tokenization:**
   - Use data masking and tokenization techniques to protect sensitive data in non-production environments. These techniques replace sensitive data with anonymized or tokenized values.

7. **Provide User Training and Awareness:**
   - Educate users about the importance of data protection and best practices for handling sensitive data. Provide regular training and awareness programs to reinforce key concepts.

8. **Maintain Compliance with Regulations:**
   - Ensure that data protection practices comply with relevant regulations and standards, such as GDPR, HIPAA, and PCI DSS. Conduct regular audits and assessments to identify and address compliance gaps.

Conclusion

In this chapter, we have explored the fundamentals of data protection, key encryption techniques and algorithms, data loss prevention (DLP) solutions, and best practices for secure data storage and transmission. Data protection is a critical aspect of an organization's cybersecurity strategy, and implementing effective measures is essential for ensuring confidentiality, integrity, and compliance. As we move forward in the subsequent chapters, we will delve deeper into specific aspects of cybersecurity, including cloud security, application security, incident response, and more. By understanding and applying the principles and best practices of data protection and encryption, organizations can enhance their resilience against cyber threats and safeguard their sensitive information.

CHAPTER 10:
CLOUD SECURITY

Overview

Cloud computing has revolutionized the way organizations operate by providing scalable, flexible, and cost-effective computing resources. However, the adoption of cloud services also introduces new security challenges and risks. Cloud security involves implementing measures and best practices to protect data, applications, and infrastructure in cloud environments. This chapter explores the fundamentals of cloud security, key cloud service models and deployment types, cloud security challenges, best practices for securing cloud environments, and cloud security compliance.

Introduction to Cloud Computing

Cloud computing is the delivery of computing resources, such as servers, storage, databases, networking, software, and analytics, over the internet ("the cloud"). Cloud computing allows organizations to access and use these resources on-demand, without the need to invest in and maintain physical infrastructure. Key characteristics of cloud computing include:

1. **On-Demand Self-Service:**
   - Users can provision and manage computing resources without human intervention from the cloud service provider.

2. **Broad Network Access:**
   - Cloud services are accessible over the internet from a wide range of devices, such as laptops,

smartphones, and tablets.

3. **Resource Pooling:**
   ○ Cloud service providers pool computing resources to serve multiple users, with resources dynamically allocated and reallocated based on demand.

4. **Rapid Elasticity:**
   ○ Cloud resources can be quickly scaled up or down to meet changing demand, providing flexibility and cost efficiency.

5. **Measured Service:**
   ○ Cloud usage is monitored, controlled, and reported, allowing users to pay only for the resources they consume.

Cloud Service Models

Cloud service models define the level of control and responsibility shared between the cloud service provider and the customer. The three primary cloud service models are:

1. **Infrastructure as a Service (IaaS):**
   ○ **Description:** IaaS provides virtualized computing resources over the internet, such as virtual machines, storage, and networking. Customers have control over the operating systems, applications, and configurations but rely on the provider for the underlying infrastructure.
   ○ **Examples:** Amazon Web Services (AWS) EC2, Microsoft Azure Virtual Machines, Google Cloud Compute Engine.

2. **Platform as a Service (PaaS):**
   ○ **Description:** PaaS provides a platform for developing, testing, and deploying applications without the need to manage

the underlying infrastructure. Customers focus on application development while the provider manages the infrastructure, middleware, and runtime.

- **Examples:** Google App Engine, Microsoft Azure App Service, Heroku.

3. **Software as a Service (SaaS):**

- **Description:** SaaS delivers software applications over the internet on a subscription basis. Customers access and use the software through a web browser, while the provider manages the underlying infrastructure, platforms, and software maintenance.

- **Examples:** Salesforce, Microsoft Office 365, Google Workspace.

Cloud Deployment Models

Cloud deployment models define how cloud services are deployed and accessed. The four primary cloud deployment models are:

1. **Public Cloud:**

- **Description:** Public cloud services are delivered over the internet and shared among multiple organizations. Public cloud providers manage and maintain the infrastructure, and customers access resources on a pay-as-you-go basis.

- **Examples:** Amazon Web Services (AWS), Microsoft Azure, Google Cloud Platform (GCP).

2. **Private Cloud:**

- **Description:** Private cloud services are dedicated to a single organization and can be hosted on-premises or by a third-party provider. Private clouds offer greater control, security, and customization but may require significant investment and management.

- **Examples:** VMware vSphere, Microsoft Azure Stack, OpenStack.

3. **Hybrid Cloud:**
   - **Description:** Hybrid cloud combines public and private cloud environments, allowing data and applications to move between them. This approach provides greater flexibility, scalability, and cost efficiency while maintaining control over sensitive data.
   - **Examples:** AWS Outposts, Microsoft Azure Arc, Google Anthos.

4. **Community Cloud:**
   - **Description:** Community cloud services are shared among organizations with common requirements, such as security, compliance, or industry standards. Community clouds can be managed by one or more of the participating organizations or by a third-party provider.
   - **Examples:** Government cloud platforms, healthcare cloud services, financial services cloud environments.

Cloud Security Challenges and Risks

1. **Data Breaches:**
   - Unauthorized access to sensitive data stored in the cloud can result in data breaches, leading to financial losses, reputational damage, and regulatory penalties.

2. **Data Loss:**
   - Data stored in the cloud can be lost due to accidental deletion, hardware failures, or

cyberattacks. Data loss can impact business continuity and recovery.

3. **Insider Threats:**
   - Malicious or negligent insiders, such as employees or contractors, can compromise cloud security by misusing their access privileges or failing to follow security policies.

4. **Insecure Interfaces and APIs:**
   - Cloud services are accessed through application programming interfaces (APIs) and interfaces. Insecure or poorly designed APIs can expose vulnerabilities and increase the risk of attacks.

5. **Misconfigurations:**
   - Incorrectly configured cloud resources, such as storage buckets, security groups, and access controls, can expose data and applications to unauthorized access and attacks.

6. **Compliance and Regulatory Concerns:**
   - Organizations must ensure that their use of cloud services complies with relevant regulations and industry standards. Non-compliance can result in legal and financial penalties.

Best Practices for Securing Cloud Environments

1. **Implement Strong Access Controls:**
   - Use strong authentication mechanisms, such as multi-factor authentication (MFA), to verify the identity of users accessing cloud resources. Implement role-based access control (RBAC) to grant access based on user roles and responsibilities.

2. **Encrypt Data at Rest and in Transit:**

○ Use encryption to protect sensitive data stored in the cloud and transmitted over the internet. Use strong encryption algorithms, such as AES for symmetric encryption and RSA for asymmetric encryption.

3. **Regularly Monitor and Audit Cloud Resources:**

   ○ Continuously monitor cloud resources for suspicious activities, misconfigurations, and compliance violations. Use security information and event management (SIEM) tools to analyze and correlate log data.

4. **Implement Secure API Management:**

   ○ Use secure API gateways and management solutions to protect cloud APIs and interfaces. Implement rate limiting, authentication, and authorization to control access to APIs.

5. **Use Cloud Security Services and Tools:**

   ○ Leverage cloud security services and tools provided by cloud service providers, such as AWS Security Hub, Azure Security Center, and Google Cloud Security Command Center. These tools offer security monitoring, threat detection, and compliance management.

6. **Conduct Regular Security Assessments:**

   ○ Perform regular security assessments, including vulnerability scans, penetration tests, and configuration audits, to identify and address potential weaknesses in cloud environments.

7. **Implement Data Backup and Recovery:**

   ○ Regularly back up data stored in the cloud to protect against data loss. Implement data recovery procedures to ensure business continuity in the event of a cyberattack or other disruption.

8. **Educate and Train Employees:**
   - Provide regular cybersecurity training and awareness programs for employees to educate them about cloud security best practices, common threats, and their role in protecting cloud resources.

Cloud Security Compliance

Compliance with regulatory requirements and industry standards is essential for organizations using cloud services. Key regulations and standards related to cloud security include:

1. **General Data Protection Regulation (GDPR):**
   - GDPR is a comprehensive data protection regulation that applies to organizations processing personal data of individuals in the European Union. It mandates strict requirements for data protection, privacy, and breach notification.

2. **Health Insurance Portability and Accountability Act (HIPAA):**
   - HIPAA is a U.S. regulation that sets standards for the protection of health information. It requires healthcare organizations to implement measures to ensure the confidentiality, integrity, and availability of patient data.

3. **Payment Card Industry Data Security Standard (PCI DSS):**
   - PCI DSS is a set of security standards designed to protect payment card information. It applies to organizations that handle cardholder data and mandates specific security controls and practices.

4. **Federal Risk and Authorization Management Program (FedRAMP):**

   ◦ FedRAMP is a U.S. government program that provides a standardized approach to security assessment, authorization, and continuous monitoring for cloud products and services used by federal agencies.

5. **ISO/IEC 27001:**

   ◦ ISO/IEC 27001 is an international standard for information security management systems (ISMS). It provides a systematic approach to managing sensitive company information and ensuring its security.

Conclusion

In this chapter, we have explored the fundamentals of cloud security, key cloud service models and deployment types, cloud security challenges, best practices for securing cloud environments, and cloud security compliance. Cloud security is a critical aspect of an organization's cybersecurity strategy, and implementing effective measures is essential for protecting data, applications, and infrastructure in cloud environments. As we move forward in the subsequent chapters, we will delve deeper into specific aspects of cybersecurity, including application security, incident response, security operations centers, and more. By understanding and applying the principles and best practices of cloud security, organizations can enhance their resilience against cyber threats and safeguard their cloud resources.

CHAPTER 11: APPLICATION SECURITY

Overview

Application security is a critical aspect of cybersecurity that focuses on protecting software applications from threats and vulnerabilities. As applications become increasingly interconnected and accessible over the internet, they become prime targets for cyberattacks. Ensuring the security of applications is essential to protect sensitive data, maintain user trust, and comply with regulatory requirements. This chapter explores the fundamentals of application security, the Secure Software Development Lifecycle (SDLC), common application vulnerabilities, web application firewalls (WAFs), and best practices for secure coding.

Fundamentals of Application Security

Application security involves implementing measures and controls to protect software applications from threats and vulnerabilities throughout their lifecycle. Key principles of application security include:

1. **Confidentiality:**
   - Ensuring that sensitive data processed or stored by applications is accessible only to authorized users and systems. Confidentiality is maintained through encryption, access controls, and secure communication

protocols.

2. **Integrity:**
   ◦ Ensuring that data processed or stored by applications remains accurate, complete, and unaltered. Integrity is maintained through hashing, digital signatures, and integrity checks.

3. **Availability:**
   ◦ Ensuring that applications and their data are available to authorized users when needed. Availability is achieved through redundancy, fault tolerance, and robust application design.

4. **Authentication:**
   ◦ Verifying the identity of users and systems before granting access to application resources. Authentication is implemented through passwords, biometrics, multi-factor authentication, and digital certificates.

5. **Authorization:**
   ◦ Granting access to application resources based on predefined policies and user roles. Authorization is enforced through access control lists (ACLs), role-based access control (RBAC), and attribute-based access control (ABAC).

6. **Accounting (Auditing):**
   ◦ Tracking and recording user activities within applications for auditing and accountability purposes. This includes logging access attempts, changes to permissions, and other relevant actions.

Secure Software Development Lifecycle (SDLC)

The Secure Software Development Lifecycle (SDLC) is a

systematic approach to integrating security into the software development process. The SDLC consists of several phases, each with specific security activities and objectives:

1. **Requirements:**
   - **Description:** Identify and document security requirements based on business needs, regulatory requirements, and threat modeling. Security requirements should address confidentiality, integrity, availability, authentication, and authorization.
   - **Activities:** Conduct threat modeling, define security policies, and establish security metrics.

2. **Design:**
   - **Description:** Create a secure application design that addresses the identified security requirements and threats. Design security controls to mitigate risks and ensure secure architecture.
   - **Activities:** Conduct security architecture reviews, design secure communication protocols, and implement access controls.

3. **Development:**
   - **Description:** Implement security controls during the coding phase to prevent vulnerabilities. Follow secure coding practices and use static code analysis tools to identify and address security issues.
   - **Activities:** Use secure coding guidelines, conduct code reviews, and perform static code analysis.

4. **Testing:**
   - **Description:** Test the application for security

vulnerabilities using dynamic analysis, penetration testing, and vulnerability scanning. Verify that security controls are functioning as intended.

  ◦ **Activities:** Conduct security testing, perform penetration testing, and use vulnerability scanners.

5. **Deployment:**

  ◦ **Description:** Deploy the application in a secure environment and ensure that security controls are properly configured. Monitor the application for security incidents and vulnerabilities.

  ◦ **Activities:** Implement secure configuration management, conduct deployment reviews, and monitor application security.

6. **Maintenance:**

  ◦ **Description:** Continuously monitor and maintain the application's security throughout its lifecycle. Apply security patches, conduct regular security assessments, and respond to security incidents.

  ◦ **Activities:** Perform regular security assessments, apply patches and updates, and monitor for security incidents.

Common Application Vulnerabilities

Applications are susceptible to various types of vulnerabilities that can be exploited by attackers. Common application vulnerabilities include:

1. **Injection Attacks:**

  ◦ **Description:** Injection attacks occur when untrusted data is sent to an interpreter as part of a command or query. Attackers can inject malicious code into the application, leading to unauthorized access or data manipulation.

- **Examples:** SQL injection, command injection, LDAP injection.

2. **Cross-Site Scripting (XSS):**

- **Description:** XSS attacks occur when an application includes untrusted data in its web pages without proper validation or escaping. Attackers can execute malicious scripts in the victim's browser, leading to data theft or session hijacking.

- **Examples:** Stored XSS, reflected XSS, DOM-based XSS.

3. **Cross-Site Request Forgery (CSRF):**

- **Description:** CSRF attacks occur when an attacker tricks a victim into performing actions on a web application without their knowledge. The attack leverages the victim's authenticated session with the application.

- **Examples:** Unauthorized fund transfers, changing account settings, performing actions on behalf of the user.

4. **Insecure Direct Object References (IDOR):**

- **Description:** IDOR vulnerabilities occur when an application exposes direct references to internal objects, such as files or database records, without proper access controls. Attackers can manipulate the references to access unauthorized data.

- **Examples:** Accessing other users' accounts, viewing sensitive files, modifying database records.

5. **Security Misconfigurations:**
   - **Description:** Security misconfigurations occur when an application or its environment is improperly configured, leading to security weaknesses. Misconfigurations can result from default settings, incomplete setups, or missing patches.
   - **Examples:** Default credentials, exposed sensitive directories, unpatched software.

6. **Sensitive Data Exposure:**
   - **Description:** Sensitive data exposure occurs when an application fails to adequately protect sensitive information, such as credit card numbers, social security numbers, or login credentials. Attackers can intercept or steal the data.
   - **Examples:** Unencrypted data transmission, insufficient encryption, improper data storage.

Web Application Firewalls (WAFs)

A Web Application Firewall (WAF) is a security solution designed to protect web applications from attacks by filtering and monitoring HTTP traffic between the application and the internet. WAFs provide an additional layer of security by detecting and blocking malicious requests. Key features of WAFs include:

1. **Traffic Filtering:**
   - WAFs analyze incoming and outgoing HTTP traffic to detect and block malicious requests based on predefined rules and policies.

2. **Protection Against OWASP Top 10:**
   - WAFs provide protection against common web application vulnerabilities, such as those

listed in the OWASP Top 10 (e.g., injection, XSS, CSRF).

3. **Custom Rules and Policies:**
   - WAFs allow organizations to create custom rules and policies to address specific security requirements and threats.

4. **Rate Limiting:**
   - WAFs can enforce rate limiting to prevent denial-of-service (DoS) attacks by limiting the number of requests from a single IP address or user.

5. **Logging and Monitoring:**
   - WAFs log and monitor HTTP traffic, providing detailed visibility into web application activity and security events.

Best Practices for Secure Coding

Secure coding practices help developers create secure applications by preventing vulnerabilities and ensuring the implementation of security controls. Best practices for secure coding include:

1. **Input Validation:**
   - Validate all input data to ensure it meets expected formats, types, and ranges. Use whitelisting techniques to allow only known good data.

2. **Output Encoding:**
   - Encode output data to prevent injection attacks, such as XSS and SQL injection. Use context-specific encoding for HTML, URL, and JavaScript.

3. **Authentication and Authorization:**
   - Implement strong authentication mechanisms, such as multi-factor

authentication (MFA), and enforce proper authorization controls based on user roles and permissions.

4. **Secure Session Management:**
   - Use secure session management techniques, such as generating unique session IDs, setting secure cookies, and implementing session timeouts.

5. **Error Handling and Logging:**
   - Implement proper error handling to prevent the disclosure of sensitive information in error messages. Log security-relevant events for auditing and monitoring purposes.

6. **Use Security Libraries and Frameworks:**
   - Leverage security libraries and frameworks to implement common security features, such as encryption, authentication, and input validation. Avoid reinventing the wheel.

7. **Regular Security Testing:**
   - Conduct regular security testing, including static code analysis, dynamic analysis, and penetration testing, to identify and address vulnerabilities.

8. **Keep Dependencies Up to Date:**
   - Regularly update third-party libraries and dependencies to address known vulnerabilities. Use dependency management tools to track and manage updates.

9. **Implement Security Headers:**
   - Use security headers, such as Content Security Policy (CSP), X-Content-Type-Options, and X-Frame-Options, to enhance web application security.

10. **Educate Developers:**

- Provide regular training and awareness programs for developers to educate them about secure coding practices and common vulnerabilities. Encourage a security-first mindset.

Conclusion

In this chapter, we have explored the fundamentals of application security, the Secure Software Development Lifecycle (SDLC), common application vulnerabilities, web application firewalls (WAFs), and best practices for secure coding. Application security is a critical aspect of an organization's cybersecurity strategy, and implementing effective measures is essential for protecting software applications from threats and vulnerabilities. As we move forward in the subsequent chapters, we will delve deeper into specific aspects of cybersecurity, including incident response, security operations centers, cybersecurity monitoring, and more. By understanding and applying the principles and best practices of application security, organizations can enhance their resilience against cyber threats and safeguard their software applications and data.

CHAPTER 12: INCIDENT RESPONSE AND MANAGEMENT

Overview

Incident response and management are critical components of an organization's cybersecurity strategy. Effective incident response helps organizations detect, contain, and recover from security incidents, minimizing the impact on operations and reducing the likelihood of future incidents. This chapter explores the fundamentals of incident response, the incident response lifecycle, key roles and responsibilities, incident response planning and preparation, detection and analysis, containment and eradication, recovery, and post-incident activities.

Fundamentals of Incident Response

Incident response involves a coordinated approach to managing and addressing security incidents. Key objectives of incident response include:

1. **Detecting and Identifying Incidents:**
   - Quickly identifying and detecting security incidents to minimize their impact and prevent further damage.

2. **Containing and Mitigating Incidents:**
   - Implementing measures to contain the incident and prevent it from spreading or

causing additional harm.

3. **Eradicating the Threat:**
   - Removing the root cause of the incident, such as malware or compromised accounts, to eliminate the threat.

4. **Recovering and Restoring Services:**
   - Restoring affected systems, services, and data to normal operations as quickly as possible.

5. **Learning and Improving:**
   - Analyzing the incident to identify lessons learned and improve the organization's incident response capabilities.

Incident Response Lifecycle

The incident response lifecycle consists of several phases, each with specific activities and objectives:

1. **Preparation:**
   - **Description:** Preparation involves establishing and maintaining an incident response capability, including developing an incident response plan, defining roles and responsibilities, and conducting training and exercises.
   - **Activities:** Develop an incident response plan, establish an incident response team, conduct training and awareness programs, perform tabletop exercises.

2. **Detection and Analysis:**
   - **Description:** Detection and analysis involve identifying and analyzing potential security incidents to determine their nature, scope, and impact. This phase includes monitoring and logging activities, as well as investigating alerts and indicators of compromise.

- **Activities:** Monitor and log security events, analyze alerts and incidents, perform triage, identify indicators of compromise, assess the impact and scope of the incident.

3. **Containment, Eradication, and Recovery:**

   - **Description:** Containment, eradication, and recovery involve taking action to contain the incident, remove the root cause, and restore affected systems and services to normal operations. This phase aims to minimize the impact and prevent further damage.

   - **Activities:** Implement containment measures, eradicate the threat, perform system and data recovery, validate the effectiveness of remediation efforts, monitor for signs of reinfection.

4. **Post-Incident Activities:**

   - **Description:** Post-incident activities involve reviewing and analyzing the incident to identify lessons learned and improve the organization's incident response capabilities. This phase includes conducting post-incident reviews, updating incident response plans, and sharing findings with stakeholders.

   - **Activities:** Conduct post-incident reviews, update incident response plans and procedures, document lessons learned, implement improvements, share findings with stakeholders.

Key Roles and Responsibilities

Effective incident response requires clear roles and responsibilities to ensure a coordinated and efficient response. Key roles in incident response include:

1. **Incident Response Team (IRT):**

- **Description:** The incident response team is responsible for managing and coordinating the response to security incidents. The team includes individuals with expertise in various areas, such as IT, cybersecurity, legal, and communications.
- **Responsibilities:** Detect and analyze incidents, implement containment and eradication measures, coordinate recovery efforts, conduct post-incident reviews.

2. **Incident Commander:**

- **Description:** The incident commander is the leader of the incident response team and is responsible for making critical decisions, coordinating response activities, and communicating with stakeholders.
- **Responsibilities:** Lead the incident response team, make key decisions, coordinate response activities, communicate with executive management and stakeholders.

3. **IT and Security Staff:**

- **Description:** IT and security staff provide technical expertise and support during incident response. They assist with detection, analysis, containment, eradication, and recovery efforts.
- **Responsibilities:** Monitor and analyze security events, implement containment measures, remove threats, restore systems and data, provide technical support.

4. **Legal and Compliance:**

- **Description:** Legal and compliance professionals ensure that the organization's incident response activities comply with relevant laws, regulations, and industry standards. They provide legal advice and support during incident response.

- **Responsibilities:** Provide legal advice, ensure compliance with regulations, support communication with regulatory authorities, assist with documentation and reporting.

5. **Communications:**

   - **Description:** Communications professionals manage internal and external communication during and after a security incident. They ensure that accurate and timely information is shared with stakeholders, including employees, customers, and the media.

   - **Responsibilities:** Develop and execute communication plans, coordinate internal and external communication, manage media relations, provide updates to stakeholders.

Incident Response Planning and Preparation

Effective incident response requires thorough planning and preparation. Key steps in incident response planning and preparation include:

1. **Develop an Incident Response Plan:**

   - **Description:** Develop a comprehensive incident response plan that outlines the procedures and protocols for detecting, responding to, and recovering from security incidents. The plan should include roles and responsibilities, communication protocols, and escalation procedures.

   - **Activities:** Define incident types and severity levels, establish incident response procedures, create communication and escalation protocols, document roles and responsibilities.

2. **Establish an Incident Response Team:**
   - **Description:** Establish a dedicated incident response team with the necessary skills and expertise to manage and coordinate incident response activities. The team should include representatives from IT, security, legal, compliance, and communications.
   - **Activities:** Identify team members, define roles and responsibilities, provide training and resources, establish incident response procedures.

3. **Conduct Training and Awareness Programs:**
   - **Description:** Provide regular training and awareness programs for employees and stakeholders to educate them about incident response procedures, common threats, and their roles in incident response.
   - **Activities:** Conduct training sessions, distribute awareness materials, perform tabletop exercises, simulate incident scenarios.

4. **Perform Tabletop Exercises and Simulations:**
   - **Description:** Conduct tabletop exercises and simulations to test the effectiveness of the incident response plan and procedures. These exercises help identify gaps and areas for improvement.
   - **Activities:** Develop exercise scenarios, conduct tabletop exercises, evaluate performance, identify areas for improvement, update the incident response plan.

Detection and Analysis

The detection and analysis phase involves identifying and analyzing potential security incidents to determine their nature, scope, and impact. Key activities in this phase include:

1. **Monitoring and Logging:**
    - **Description:** Continuously monitor security events and activities using security information and event management (SIEM) tools, intrusion detection systems (IDS), and other monitoring solutions. Log relevant events for analysis and investigation.
    - **Activities:** Monitor security events, collect and analyze log data, identify anomalies and suspicious activities, generate alerts.

2. **Triage and Prioritization:**
    - **Description:** Perform triage to prioritize incidents based on their severity, impact, and urgency. Categorize incidents to determine the appropriate response and escalation.
    - **Activities:** Assess incident severity and impact, categorize incidents, prioritize response efforts, escalate critical incidents.

3. **Incident Investigation and Analysis:**
    - **Description:** Investigate and analyze incidents to determine their root cause, scope, and impact. Identify indicators of compromise (IOCs) and gather evidence for remediation and reporting.
    - **Activities:** Investigate incidents, analyze attack vectors, identify IOCs, gather evidence, assess impact and scope.

Containment, Eradication, and Recovery

The containment, eradication, and recovery phase involves taking action to contain the incident, remove the root cause, and restore affected systems and services. Key activities in this phase include:

1. **Containment:**
   - **Description:** Implement containment measures to prevent the incident from spreading or causing further damage. Containment strategies can be short-term or long-term, depending on the severity and impact of the incident.
   - **Activities:** Isolate affected systems, block malicious traffic, disable compromised accounts, implement network segmentation.

2. **Eradication:**
   - **Description:** Remove the root cause of the incident, such as malware, compromised accounts, or vulnerabilities. Ensure that the threat is completely eliminated to prevent reinfection.
   - **Activities:** Remove malware, patch vulnerabilities, reset credentials, clean affected systems, validate eradication efforts.

3. **Recovery:**
   - **Description:** Restore affected systems, services, and data to normal operations. Validate the integrity and functionality of restored systems and monitor for signs of reinfection.
   - **Activities:** Restore data from backups, rebuild systems, validate system functionality, monitor for signs of reinfection.

Post-Incident Activities

Post-incident activities involve reviewing and analyzing the incident to identify lessons learned and improve the organization's incident response capabilities. Key activities in this phase include:

1. **Post-Incident Review:**
   - **Description:** Conduct a post-incident review to analyze the incident and the effectiveness of the response. Identify strengths, weaknesses, and areas for improvement.
   - **Activities:** Review incident details, evaluate response performance, identify lessons learned, document findings.

2. **Updating Incident Response Plans:**
   - **Description:** Update the incident response plan and procedures based on the findings from the post-incident review. Ensure that the plan reflects the lessons learned and addresses identified gaps.
   - **Activities:** Revise incident response plan, update procedures, incorporate lessons learned, communicate updates to stakeholders.

3. **Documenting Lessons Learned:**
   - **Description:** Document the lessons learned from the incident to improve the organization's incident response capabilities and prevent similar incidents in the future.
   - **Activities:** Document lessons learned, share findings with stakeholders, implement corrective actions, update training and awareness programs.

4.

continue

4. **Implementing Improvements:**
   - **Description:** Implement the improvements

and corrective actions identified during the post-incident review. This may involve updating security controls, enhancing monitoring capabilities, and refining incident response procedures.

- **Activities:** Implement corrective actions, update security controls, enhance monitoring, refine incident response procedures.

5. **Sharing Findings with Stakeholders:**

- **Description:** Communicate the findings and lessons learned from the incident to relevant stakeholders, including executive management, IT staff, and legal and compliance teams. This ensures that everyone is aware of the incident's impact and the steps taken to prevent future incidents.

- **Activities:** Prepare incident reports, conduct briefings and meetings, share lessons learned, discuss improvements.

Conclusion

In this chapter, we have explored the fundamentals of incident response and management, the incident response lifecycle, key roles and responsibilities, incident response planning and preparation, detection and analysis, containment and eradication, recovery, and post-incident activities. Effective incident response is essential for minimizing the impact of security incidents, maintaining business continuity, and improving an organization's overall cybersecurity posture. By understanding and applying the principles and best practices of incident response, organizations can enhance their resilience against cyber threats and ensure a swift and coordinated response to security incidents.

As we move forward in the subsequent chapters, we will delve deeper into specific aspects of cybersecurity, including security operations centers, cybersecurity monitoring and analytics, vulnerability management, and more. By continuing to build on the knowledge and practices discussed in this chapter, organizations can strengthen their cybersecurity defenses and better protect their information assets from evolving threats.

CHAPTER 13:
CLOUD SECURITY

Overview

Cloud security is a critical aspect of modern cybersecurity, focusing on protecting data, applications, and services hosted in cloud environments from threats and vulnerabilities. As organizations increasingly adopt cloud services for their scalability, flexibility, and cost-efficiency, ensuring the security of cloud infrastructure becomes paramount. This chapter explores the fundamentals of cloud security, common threats and vulnerabilities, best practices for securing cloud environments, compliance and regulatory considerations, and the future of cloud security.

Fundamentals of Cloud Security

Cloud security involves implementing measures and controls to protect cloud-based systems, data, and infrastructure from threats. Key principles of cloud security include:

1. **Confidentiality:**
   - Ensuring that sensitive data stored, processed, or transmitted in the cloud is accessible only to authorized users and systems. Confidentiality is maintained through encryption, access controls, and secure communication protocols.

2. **Integrity:**
   - Ensuring that data stored or processed in the cloud remains accurate, complete, and

unaltered. Integrity is maintained through hashing, digital signatures, and integrity checks.

3. **Availability:**
   ◦ Ensuring that cloud services and data are available to authorized users when needed. Availability is achieved through redundancy, fault tolerance, and robust cloud architecture.

4. **Authentication:**
   ◦ Verifying the identity of users and systems before granting access to cloud resources. Authentication is implemented through passwords, multi-factor authentication (MFA), and identity management solutions.

5. **Authorization:**
   ◦ Granting access to cloud resources based on predefined policies and user roles. Authorization is enforced through access control lists (ACLs), role-based access control (RBAC), and attribute-based access control (ABAC).

6. **Accountability (Auditing):**
   ◦ Tracking and recording user activities within cloud environments for auditing and accountability purposes. This includes logging access attempts, changes to permissions, and other relevant actions.

Common Cloud Security Threats and Vulnerabilities

Cloud environments are susceptible to various threats and vulnerabilities that can compromise the security of data and services. Common cloud security threats and vulnerabilities include:

1. **Data Breaches:**

- **Description:** Unauthorized access to sensitive data stored in the cloud, often resulting in data theft, exposure, or loss. Data breaches can occur due to weak access controls, misconfigurations, or vulnerabilities in cloud applications.
- **Examples:** Unauthorized access to customer data, theft of intellectual property, exposure of confidential business information.

2. **Misconfigurations:**

- **Description:** Incorrect configuration of cloud resources and services, leading to security weaknesses and vulnerabilities. Misconfigurations can result from human error, lack of expertise, or inadequate security practices.
- **Examples:** Publicly accessible storage buckets, misconfigured security groups, improper identity and access management (IAM) settings.

3. **Insecure APIs:**

- **Description:** Vulnerabilities in cloud application programming interfaces (APIs) that can be exploited by attackers to gain unauthorized access or perform malicious actions. Insecure APIs can result from poor coding practices, lack of authentication, or inadequate security controls.
- **Examples:** API key leakage, lack of rate limiting, insufficient input validation.

4. **Denial of Service (DoS) Attacks:**

- **Description:** Attacks that overwhelm cloud services with excessive traffic or requests, rendering them unavailable to legitimate users. DoS attacks can target specific cloud applications, services, or infrastructure components.

○ **Examples:** Distributed Denial of Service (DDoS) attacks, resource exhaustion, application-layer DoS attacks.

5. **Insider Threats:**

○ **Description:** Threats posed by malicious or negligent insiders with authorized access to cloud resources. Insider threats can result from employees, contractors, or partners who misuse their access privileges.

○ **Examples:** Data theft, unauthorized access, sabotage, accidental data exposure.

6. **Malware and Ransomware:**

○ **Description:** Malicious software that infects cloud resources, compromising data integrity, availability, and confidentiality. Malware and ransomware attacks can spread through cloud-based email, file sharing, or applications.

○ **Examples:** Ransomware encrypting cloud-hosted data, malware infecting cloud workloads, phishing attacks targeting cloud users.

Best Practices for Securing Cloud Environments

Implementing best practices for cloud security helps protect cloud environments from threats and vulnerabilities. Key best practices include:

1. **Encryption:**

○ **Description:** Encrypt data at rest and in transit to protect it from unauthorized access. Use strong encryption algorithms and key management practices.

- **Practices:** Enable encryption for cloud storage, use HTTPS/TLS for data transmission, implement key rotation and management policies.

2. **Access Controls:**

   - **Description:** Implement strict access controls to ensure that only authorized users and systems can access cloud resources. Use role-based access control (RBAC) and least privilege principles.
   - **Practices:** Define user roles and permissions, enforce multi-factor authentication (MFA), regularly review and update access policies.

3. **Security Configuration Management:**

   - **Description:** Regularly review and manage the security configuration of cloud resources to prevent misconfigurations and vulnerabilities.
   - **Practices:** Use configuration management tools, conduct regular security audits, implement automated compliance checks.

4. **Continuous Monitoring:**

   - **Description:** Continuously monitor cloud environments for security threats and incidents. Use security information and event management (SIEM) systems and automated monitoring tools.
   - **Practices:** Set up real-time alerts for suspicious activities, conduct regular vulnerability scans, monitor network traffic and access logs.

5. **Incident Response:**

- ○ **Description:** Develop and implement an incident response plan for cloud environments. Ensure timely detection, containment, and remediation of security incidents.
- ○ **Practices:** Define incident response roles and responsibilities, conduct regular incident response drills, maintain an up-to-date incident response playbook.

6. **Secure API Management:**

- ○ **Description:** Implement security controls for cloud APIs to protect them from threats and vulnerabilities.
- ○ **Practices:** Use API gateways, enforce authentication and authorization, implement rate limiting and input validation.

Compliance and Regulatory Considerations

Compliance with regulatory requirements and industry standards is essential for ensuring the security and integrity of cloud environments. Key compliance and regulatory considerations include:

1. **General Data Protection Regulation (GDPR):**

- ○ **Description:** GDPR is a comprehensive data protection regulation that applies to organizations processing personal data of EU residents. It mandates strict data protection measures and grants rights to individuals regarding their data.
- ○ **Requirements:** Implement data protection measures, obtain consent for data processing, provide data access and deletion rights, report data breaches within 72 hours.

2. **Health Insurance Portability and Accountability Act**

(HIPAA):

- **Description:** HIPAA sets standards for protecting the privacy and security of health information in the United States. It applies to healthcare providers, insurers, and their business associates.
- **Requirements:** Implement administrative, physical, and technical safeguards, ensure data confidentiality and integrity, conduct regular risk assessments, report security incidents.

3. **Payment Card Industry Data Security Standard (PCI DSS):**

- **Description:** PCI DSS is a set of security standards for organizations handling credit card transactions. It aims to protect cardholder data and prevent data breaches.
- **Requirements:** Implement strong access controls, encrypt cardholder data, maintain secure systems and applications, conduct regular security testing and monitoring.

4. **ISO/IEC 27001:**

- **Description:** ISO/IEC 27001 is an international standard for information security management systems (ISMS). It provides a systematic approach to managing sensitive information and ensuring data security.
- **Requirements:** Implement an ISMS, conduct risk assessments, establish security controls, conduct internal audits and reviews.

The Future of Cloud Security

The future of cloud security is shaped by emerging technologies, evolving threats, and changing regulatory landscapes. Key trends and innovations that will influence cloud security include:

1. **Zero Trust Architecture:**
   - **Description:** Zero Trust is a security model that assumes no implicit trust within a network, and every access request must be authenticated, authorized, and continuously monitored. It enhances security by minimizing the attack surface.
   - **Applications:** Micro-segmentation, continuous monitoring, identity and access management, least privilege access.

2. **Artificial Intelligence (AI) and Machine Learning (ML):**
   - **Description:** AI and ML technologies are increasingly used to enhance cloud security by detecting anomalies, predicting threats, and automating security responses.
   - **Applications:** Threat detection and response, behavioral analytics, automated incident response, security analytics.

3. **Serverless Computing Security:**
   - **Description:** Serverless computing allows developers to build and deploy applications without managing underlying infrastructure. Ensuring security in serverless environments requires addressing unique challenges and risks.
   - **Applications:** Secure function development, access controls, monitoring and logging, managing third-party dependencies.

4. **Blockchain for Cloud Security:**
   - **Description:** Blockchain technology offers

potential benefits for cloud security by providing secure, transparent, and tamper-resistant records. It can enhance data integrity, traceability, and trust.

- **Applications:** Secure data sharing, decentralized identity management, supply chain security, smart contracts.

5. **Quantum Computing:**

- **Description:** Quantum computing has the potential to break traditional encryption algorithms, posing challenges for cloud security. However, it also offers opportunities for developing quantum-resistant encryption and enhancing security.

- **Applications:** Quantum-resistant cryptography, secure key distribution, advanced threat detection.

Conclusion

Cloud security is a critical aspect of modern cybersecurity that requires a comprehensive approach to protect data, applications, and services in cloud environments. By understanding the fundamentals of cloud security, recognizing common threats and vulnerabilities, implementing best practices, and staying informed about compliance and regulatory considerations, organizations can enhance the security of their cloud infrastructure. As we look to the future, emerging technologies and

CHAPTER 14: EMERGING TECHNOLOGIES AND FUTURE TRENDS IN CYBERSECURITY

Overview

The cybersecurity landscape is continuously evolving, driven by the rapid advancement of technology and the increasing sophistication of cyber threats. As organizations and individuals become more reliant on digital systems and the internet, the importance of robust cybersecurity measures cannot be overstated. This chapter explores emerging technologies and future trends in cybersecurity, highlighting how they can be leveraged to enhance security and mitigate risks.

Artificial Intelligence (AI) and Machine Learning (ML)

Artificial intelligence (AI) and machine learning (ML) are revolutionizing cybersecurity by providing advanced tools and techniques to detect, prevent, and respond to cyber threats. Key applications of AI and ML in cybersecurity include:

1. **Threat Detection and Analysis:**
    - **Description:** AI and ML algorithms can analyze vast amounts of data to identify patterns and anomalies indicative of cyber

threats. These technologies can detect and respond to threats in real-time, reducing the time it takes to mitigate risks.

- **Benefits:** Improved accuracy and speed in threat detection, reduced false positives, and enhanced ability to detect previously unknown threats.

2. **Behavioral Analytics:**

- **Description:** ML models can analyze user behavior to establish baselines of normal activity and identify deviations that may indicate malicious activity. Behavioral analytics helps detect insider threats and compromised accounts.
- **Benefits:** Early detection of insider threats, enhanced security of user accounts, and reduced risk of data breaches.

3. **Automated Incident Response:**

- **Description:** AI-powered systems can automate incident response processes, enabling rapid and efficient handling of security incidents. Automated response can include actions such as isolating affected systems, blocking malicious traffic, and notifying relevant personnel.
- **Benefits:** Faster incident response times, reduced manual workload for security teams, and minimized impact of security incidents.

Blockchain Technology

Blockchain technology, known for its use in cryptocurrencies, has significant potential in enhancing cybersecurity. Key applications of blockchain in cybersecurity include:

1. **Secure Data Sharing:**

- **Description:** Blockchain's decentralized and immutable nature makes it ideal for secure data sharing. Organizations can use blockchain to securely share sensitive data without the risk of tampering or unauthorized access.
- **Benefits:** Enhanced data integrity, improved transparency, and reduced risk of data breaches.

2. **Identity and Access Management (IAM):**

- **Description:** Blockchain can be used to create decentralized and tamper-proof digital identities. This approach enhances the security of identity verification and access management processes.
- **Benefits:** Reduced risk of identity theft, improved security of authentication processes, and enhanced user privacy.

3. **Supply Chain Security:**

- **Description:** Blockchain can enhance supply chain security by providing a transparent and immutable record of transactions and product movements. This helps detect and prevent counterfeit products and ensures the integrity of the supply chain.
- **Benefits:** Improved traceability, reduced risk of fraud, and enhanced supply chain transparency.

Quantum Computing

Quantum computing has the potential to revolutionize cybersecurity, both as a threat and an opportunity. Key aspects of quantum computing in cybersecurity include:

1. **Quantum-Resistant Cryptography:**

- **Description:** Quantum computers have the potential to break traditional encryption algorithms, posing a significant threat to data security. To mitigate this risk, researchers are developing quantum-resistant cryptographic algorithms that can withstand quantum attacks.
- **Benefits:** Enhanced security of encrypted data, protection against future quantum threats, and continued trust in cryptographic systems.

2. **Quantum Key Distribution (QKD):**

- **Description:** QKD leverages the principles of quantum mechanics to securely distribute encryption keys. QKD provides an unbreakable method for key exchange, ensuring secure communication.
- **Benefits:** Unbreakable encryption key exchange, enhanced security of communication channels, and reduced risk of key interception.

3. **Quantum Computing for Threat Detection:**

- **Description:** Quantum computers can process vast amounts of data at unprecedented speeds, making them valuable tools for threat detection and analysis. Quantum computing can enhance the ability to detect and respond to complex cyber threats.
- **Benefits:** Improved threat detection capabilities, faster analysis of large datasets, and enhanced ability to identify sophisticated attacks.

Internet of Things (IoT) Security

The proliferation of IoT devices presents new cybersecurity

challenges and opportunities. Securing IoT environments is critical to protect against potential threats. Key aspects of IoT security include:

1. **Device Authentication and Authorization:**
   - ◦ **Description:** Implementing strong authentication and authorization mechanisms for IoT devices ensures that only legitimate devices can access the network and perform actions.
   - ◦ **Benefits:** Reduced risk of unauthorized access, improved security of IoT networks, and enhanced trust in connected devices.

2. **Endpoint Security:**
   - ◦ **Description:** Securing IoT endpoints involves protecting the devices themselves from vulnerabilities and attacks. This includes implementing security measures such as encryption, secure boot, and firmware updates.
   - ◦ **Benefits:** Enhanced security of IoT devices, reduced risk of device compromise, and improved overall network security.

3. **Network Segmentation:**
   - ◦ **Description:** Segmenting IoT networks from other critical networks helps contain potential security incidents and prevent the spread of threats.
   - ◦ **Benefits:** Improved containment of security incidents, reduced risk of lateral movement, and enhanced overall network security.

5G Security

The rollout of 5G networks brings new security challenges and opportunities. Ensuring the security of 5G infrastructure and services is essential to protect against potential threats. Key aspects of 5G security include:

1. **Enhanced Encryption:**
   - **Description:** 5G networks utilize advanced encryption algorithms to protect data transmitted over the network. This ensures the confidentiality and integrity of communication.
   - **Benefits:** Improved security of data in transit, enhanced protection against eavesdropping, and reduced risk of data breaches.

2. **Network Slicing:**
   - **Description:** Network slicing allows the creation of virtual networks within a 5G network, each with its own security policies and configurations. This enables customized security measures for different use cases.
   - **Benefits:** Enhanced security of virtual networks, improved resource allocation, and increased flexibility in network management.

3. **Edge Computing Security:**
   - **Description:** 5G networks enable edge computing, where data processing occurs closer to the source. Ensuring the security of edge computing environments is critical to protect against potential threats.
   - **Benefits:** Reduced latency, improved data security, and enhanced scalability of IoT and other applications.

Conclusion

Emerging technologies and future trends in cybersecurity offer new opportunities to enhance security, mitigate risks, and address evolving threats. By leveraging advanced tools such as

AI and ML, blockchain technology, quantum computing, IoT security measures, and 5G security practices, organizations can stay ahead of cyber threats and protect their digital assets. As the cybersecurity landscape continues to evolve, staying informed about these trends and adopting innovative solutions will be essential for building a secure and resilient digital future.

By exploring the topics covered in this chapter, readers will gain valuable insights into the potential of emerging technologies to transform cybersecurity and ensure the protection of critical data and systems. As we look to the future, it is clear that continued innovation and collaboration will be key to addressing the complex challenges of the cybersecurity landscape.

CHAPTER 15: CAREER PATHS IN CYBERSECURITY

Introduction

The field of cybersecurity offers diverse and rewarding career opportunities for individuals with various skill sets and interests. As cyber threats continue to evolve and become more sophisticated, the demand for skilled cybersecurity professionals is on the rise. This chapter explores the different career paths in cybersecurity, the skills and qualifications required for each role, and tips for building a successful career in this dynamic and critical field.

Common Cybersecurity Career Paths

1. **Security Analyst:**

   ◦ **Description:** Security analysts are responsible for monitoring and analyzing an organization's security systems, identifying vulnerabilities, and responding to security incidents. They implement security measures to protect data and systems from cyber threats.

   ◦ **Key Responsibilities:** Conducting security assessments, monitoring network traffic, analyzing security breaches, implementing security controls, and generating reports.

- **Skills and Qualifications:** Knowledge of network security, intrusion detection systems (IDS), security information and event management (SIEM) tools, and incident response. Certifications such as CompTIA Security+, Certified Information Systems Security Professional (CISSP), and Certified Ethical Hacker (CEH) are beneficial.

2. **Penetration Tester (Ethical Hacker):**
    - **Description:** Penetration testers, also known as ethical hackers, are responsible for simulating cyberattacks on an organization's systems to identify and exploit vulnerabilities. They provide recommendations to improve security posture.
    - **Key Responsibilities:** Conducting penetration tests, identifying security weaknesses, creating detailed vulnerability reports, and collaborating with IT teams to remediate issues.
    - **Skills and Qualifications:** Proficiency in hacking techniques, vulnerability assessment tools, and penetration testing methodologies. Certifications such as Offensive Security Certified Professional (OSCP), Certified Ethical Hacker (CEH), and GIAC Penetration Tester (GPEN) are valuable.

3. **Security Engineer:**
    - **Description:** Security engineers design, implement, and maintain an organization's security infrastructure. They develop and deploy security solutions to protect against cyber threats and ensure compliance with

security policies.

- **Key Responsibilities:** Designing and implementing security architectures, configuring security tools, conducting security audits, and performing risk assessments.
- **Skills and Qualifications:** Strong knowledge of network security, encryption, firewalls, intrusion prevention systems (IPS), and security protocols. Certifications such as CISSP, Certified Information Security Manager (CISM), and Cisco Certified Network Associate (CCNA) Security are advantageous.

4. **Incident Responder:**

- **Description:** Incident responders are responsible for managing and responding to security incidents, such as data breaches and cyberattacks. They investigate incidents, contain threats, and develop strategies to prevent future occurrences.
- **Key Responsibilities:** Investigating security incidents, containing and mitigating threats, conducting forensic analysis, and documenting incident response activities.
- **Skills and Qualifications:** Knowledge of digital forensics, malware analysis, incident response procedures, and security operations center (SOC) tools. Certifications such as Certified Incident Handler (CIH), GIAC Certified Incident Handler (GCIH), and Certified Forensic Computer Examiner (CFCE) are beneficial.

5. **Security Architect:**

- **Description:** Security architects are

responsible for designing and overseeing the implementation of an organization's security infrastructure. They develop security strategies, assess risks, and ensure the security of systems and data.

- **Key Responsibilities:** Designing security architectures, developing security policies, conducting risk assessments, and providing guidance on security best practices.
- **Skills and Qualifications:** Extensive knowledge of security frameworks, network architecture, cryptography, and security risk management. Certifications such as CISSP, Certified Information Systems Auditor (CISA), and Certified Cloud Security Professional (CCSP) are valuable.

6. **Chief Information Security Officer (CISO):**
    - **Description:** The CISO is a senior executive responsible for overseeing an organization's information security strategy and operations. They lead the security team, develop security policies, and ensure compliance with regulatory requirements.
    - **Key Responsibilities:** Developing and implementing security strategies, managing security budgets, leading security teams, and communicating with stakeholders about security risks and initiatives.
    - **Skills and Qualifications:** Strong leadership skills, knowledge of security frameworks, risk management, compliance, and strategic planning. Certifications such as CISSP, CISM, and Certified Chief Information Security Officer (CCISO) are advantageous.

Skills and Qualifications for Cybersecurity Careers

To succeed in a cybersecurity career, individuals need a combination of technical skills, soft skills, and relevant certifications. Key skills and qualifications include:

1. **Technical Skills:**

   - **Network Security:** Understanding of network protocols, firewalls, VPNs, IDS/IPS, and network monitoring tools.
   - **Programming and Scripting:** Proficiency in programming languages such as Python, Java, C++, and scripting languages like PowerShell and Bash.
   - **Operating Systems:** Knowledge of operating systems, including Windows, Linux, and macOS, as well as their security features and configurations.
   - **Encryption and Cryptography:** Understanding of encryption algorithms, key management, and cryptographic protocols.
   - **Vulnerability Assessment:** Familiarity with vulnerability scanning tools and techniques for identifying and mitigating security weaknesses.

2. **Soft Skills:**

   - **Analytical Thinking:** Ability to analyze complex data and identify patterns and anomalies indicative of security threats.
   - **Problem-Solving:** Strong problem-solving skills to address security challenges and develop effective solutions.
   - **Communication:** Effective communication skills to convey technical information to non-technical stakeholders and collaborate with

team members.

- **Attention to Detail:** Attention to detail to identify potential security risks and ensure thorough security assessments and audits.

3. **Certifications:**

- Certifications are valuable for validating expertise and knowledge in cybersecurity. Some widely recognized certifications include:
  - CompTIA Security+
  - Certified Information Systems Security Professional (CISSP)
  - Certified Ethical Hacker (CEH)
  - Certified Information Security Manager (CISM)
  - Certified Information Systems Auditor (CISA)
  - Offensive Security Certified Professional (OSCP)
  - GIAC Security Essentials (GSEC)

Tips for Building a Successful Cybersecurity Career

Building a successful career in cybersecurity requires continuous learning, professional development, and networking. Here are some tips to help you advance in your cybersecurity career:

1. **Stay Informed:**

- Stay updated with the latest cybersecurity trends, threats, and technologies by reading industry publications, blogs, and research papers. Attend webinars, conferences, and workshops to gain insights and knowledge.

2. **Gain Practical Experience:**

- Seek opportunities to gain hands-on experience through internships, co-op programs, and volunteer work. Participate in capture-the-flag (CTF) competitions, hackathons, and cybersecurity challenges to hone your skills.

3. **Build a Professional Network:**
   - Connect with cybersecurity professionals through online forums, social media, and professional associations. Join cybersecurity organizations such as (ISC)², ISACA, and SANS Institute to expand your network and access resources.

4. **Pursue Advanced Education:**
   - Consider pursuing advanced education, such as a master's degree in cybersecurity or a related field, to deepen your knowledge and enhance your career prospects.

5. **Continuously Improve:**
   - Invest in continuous learning and professional development by obtaining relevant certifications, attending training programs, and engaging in self-study. Stay curious and proactive in expanding your skill set.

6. **Showcase Your Skills:**
   - Create a professional portfolio showcasing your cybersecurity projects, certifications, and achievements. Use platforms like GitHub to share your work and demonstrate your expertise.

Conclusion

Cybersecurity is a dynamic and rapidly evolving field that offers diverse career opportunities for individuals with a passion for technology and a commitment to protecting digital assets. By understanding the different career paths, acquiring the necessary skills and qualifications, and following best practices for career development, you can build a successful and fulfilling career in cybersecurity. As you embark on this journey, remember that continuous learning, adaptability, and a proactive approach to professional growth are key to staying ahead in the ever-changing cybersecurity landscape.

CHAPTER 16: ETHICAL HACKING AND PENETRATION TESTING

Introduction

Ethical hacking and penetration testing are critical components of cybersecurity that involve identifying and addressing security vulnerabilities in systems, networks, and applications. Ethical hackers, also known as white-hat hackers, use their skills to protect organizations from cyber threats by simulating attacks and finding weaknesses before malicious hackers can exploit them. This chapter explores the principles and practices of ethical hacking and penetration testing, including the methodologies, tools, and techniques used by ethical hackers to secure digital environments.

Principles of Ethical Hacking

Ethical hacking is guided by a set of principles that ensure the integrity and legality of the practice. Key principles of ethical hacking include:

1. **Legal Authorization:**
   - Ethical hackers must obtain explicit permission from the organization before conducting any tests or assessments. Unauthorized hacking is illegal and unethical.

2. **Integrity and Honesty:**

   ○ Ethical hackers must maintain the highest standards of integrity and honesty. They should report all findings accurately and avoid any actions that could harm the organization or its stakeholders.

3. **Confidentiality:**

   ○ Ethical hackers must keep all information obtained during the testing process confidential. They should not disclose any sensitive data to unauthorized parties.

4. **Minimizing Impact:**

   ○ Ethical hackers should conduct their activities in a way that minimizes disruption to the organization's operations. They should avoid causing any harm or damage to the systems being tested.

5. **Responsibility:**

   ○ Ethical hackers are responsible for their actions and must adhere to ethical guidelines and industry best practices. They should work to improve security and prevent malicious activities.

Methodologies for Penetration Testing

Penetration testing, also known as pen testing, involves systematically assessing the security of systems and networks by simulating real-world attacks. Common methodologies for penetration testing include:

1. **Reconnaissance:**

   ○ **Description:** The initial phase of penetration testing involves gathering information about the target system, network, or application. This phase, also known as information gathering or footprinting, helps identify potential entry points for attacks.

- **Techniques:** Passive reconnaissance (e.g., WHOIS lookup, social media analysis), active reconnaissance (e.g., network scanning, port scanning).

2. **Scanning and Enumeration:**

- **Description:** In this phase, ethical hackers use scanning tools to identify open ports, services, and vulnerabilities on the target system. Enumeration involves obtaining detailed information about the target, such as user accounts, network shares, and system configurations.
- **Techniques:** Network scanning (e.g., Nmap), vulnerability scanning (e.g., Nessus), enumeration (e.g., NetBIOS enumeration).

3. **Exploitation:**

- **Description:** Exploitation involves attempting to gain unauthorized access to the target system by exploiting identified vulnerabilities. Ethical hackers use various techniques and tools to compromise the target and gain control.
- **Techniques:** Buffer overflow attacks, SQL injection, cross-site scripting (XSS), password cracking.

4. **Post-Exploitation:**

- **Description:** After gaining access to the target system, ethical hackers perform post-exploitation activities to maintain access, escalate privileges, and gather additional information. This phase helps assess the extent of potential damage and the impact of a successful attack.

- **Techniques:** Privilege escalation, lateral movement, data exfiltration, persistence techniques.

5. **Reporting:**

- **Description:** The final phase of penetration testing involves documenting the findings, including identified vulnerabilities, exploitation techniques, and recommendations for remediation. Ethical hackers provide a detailed report to the organization to help improve security.

- **Components:** Executive summary, technical details, vulnerability descriptions, risk assessments, remediation recommendations.

Tools and Techniques Used in Ethical Hacking

Ethical hackers use a variety of tools and techniques to identify and exploit vulnerabilities in target systems. Common tools and techniques include:

1. **Scanning and Enumeration Tools:**

- **Nmap:** A network scanning tool used to discover hosts, open ports, and services on a network.

- **Nessus:** A vulnerability scanning tool that identifies security weaknesses and provides detailed reports.

- **Metasploit Framework:** A penetration testing framework that provides a comprehensive set of tools for scanning, exploitation, and post-exploitation activities.

2. **Exploitation Tools:**

- **Metasploit Framework:** Used for developing and executing exploit code against target systems.

- **Burp Suite:** A web vulnerability scanner and proxy tool used for identifying and exploiting web application vulnerabilities.
- **Hydra:** A password-cracking tool used for brute-forcing login credentials.

3. **Post-Exploitation Tools:**

- **Mimikatz:** A tool used for extracting plaintext passwords, hashes, and Kerberos tickets from memory.
- **Empire:** A post-exploitation framework for managing compromised systems and performing lateral movement.
- **BloodHound:** A tool for analyzing Active Directory environments and identifying paths for privilege escalation.

4. **Social Engineering Techniques:**

- **Phishing:** Sending fraudulent emails to trick recipients into disclosing sensitive information or downloading malicious attachments.
- **Pretexting:** Creating a fabricated scenario to manipulate individuals into providing confidential information.
- **Baiting:** Leaving physical media (e.g., USB drives) with malicious content in conspicuous locations to entice individuals to use them.

Legal and Ethical Considerations

Ethical hacking must be conducted within the boundaries of the law and ethical guidelines. Key legal and ethical considerations include:

1. **Obtaining Authorization:**

- Ethical hackers must obtain written consent

from the organization before conducting any testing activities. Unauthorized access or hacking is illegal and can result in severe penalties.

2. **Respecting Privacy:**

   ◦ Ethical hackers must respect the privacy of individuals and avoid accessing or disclosing personal or sensitive information without proper authorization.

3. **Avoiding Harm:**

   ◦ Ethical hackers should take measures to minimize the impact of their activities and avoid causing any harm or disruption to the target systems or the organization.

4. **Adhering to Ethical Guidelines:**

   ◦ Ethical hackers should adhere to industry standards and ethical guidelines, such as the EC-Council Code of Ethics and the Offensive Security Code of Ethics.

Conclusion

Ethical hacking and penetration testing play a crucial role in identifying and addressing security vulnerabilities in systems, networks, and applications. By following ethical principles, using systematic methodologies, and employing advanced tools and techniques, ethical hackers help organizations strengthen their security posture and protect against cyber threats. As the cybersecurity landscape continues to evolve, the importance of ethical hacking in proactive security measures cannot be overstated. This chapter provides a comprehensive overview of ethical hacking and penetration testing, offering valuable insights for aspiring ethical hackers and organizations seeking to enhance their cybersecurity defenses.

CHAPTER 17: INCIDENT RESPONSE AND FORENSICS

Introduction

Incident response and forensics are critical components of a comprehensive cybersecurity strategy. Incident response involves the systematic approach to managing and mitigating security incidents, while forensics focuses on the investigation and analysis of digital evidence to determine the root cause and impact of security breaches. This chapter explores the principles, processes, and best practices for incident response and forensics, helping organizations effectively handle security incidents and strengthen their cybersecurity posture.

Principles of Incident Response

Incident response is guided by a set of principles that ensure effective and efficient management of security incidents. Key principles of incident response include:

1. **Preparation:**
   - **Description:** Being prepared for security incidents by developing and maintaining an incident response plan, training staff, and establishing communication protocols.
   - **Practices:** Conduct regular training and drills, establish an incident response team (IRT), and create a comprehensive incident response

plan.

2. **Identification:**
    ◦ **Description:** Detecting and identifying potential security incidents through continuous monitoring, logging, and alerting systems.
    ◦ **Practices:** Implement intrusion detection systems (IDS), security information and event management (SIEM) solutions, and automated monitoring tools.

3. **Containment:**
    ◦ **Description:** Containing the impact of a security incident to prevent further damage and limit the spread of the threat.
    ◦ **Practices:** Isolate affected systems, disable compromised accounts, and implement network segmentation.

4. **Eradication:**
    ◦ **Description:** Removing the root cause of the security incident and eliminating any malicious artifacts from the environment.
    ◦ **Practices:** Conduct malware analysis, patch vulnerabilities, and remove compromised files and applications.

5. **Recovery:**
    ◦ **Description:** Restoring affected systems and services to normal operations while ensuring that the threat has been fully eradicated.
    ◦ **Practices:** Restore from backups, rebuild systems, and conduct post-incident testing to verify that the environment is secure.

6. **Lessons Learned:**
    ◦ **Description:** Analyzing the incident response

process to identify areas for improvement and prevent future incidents.

- ◦ **Practices:** Conduct post-incident reviews, document findings, and update the incident response plan based on lessons learned.

Incident Response Process

The incident response process consists of several key stages that ensure a structured and effective approach to handling security incidents. The stages include:

1. **Preparation:**
   - ◦ **Description:** Establishing the foundation for effective incident response by developing an incident response plan, assembling an incident response team, and conducting regular training and drills.
   - ◦ **Components:** Incident response policy, incident response plan, roles and responsibilities, communication protocols, incident response toolkit.

2. **Detection and Analysis:**
   - ◦ **Description:** Detecting potential security incidents through continuous monitoring and analyzing alerts to determine the nature and scope of the incident.
   - ◦ **Components:** Monitoring and logging systems, SIEM solutions, threat intelligence feeds, incident classification, and prioritization.

3. **Containment:**
   - ◦ **Description:** Containing the incident to prevent further damage and limit the spread of the threat. Containment strategies can be short-term (immediate) or long-term

(sustained).

- ○ **Components:** Isolation of affected systems, disabling compromised accounts, network segmentation, and communication protocols.

4. **Eradication:**
   - ○ **Description:** Eliminating the root cause of the incident and removing any malicious artifacts from the environment. This stage ensures that the threat is fully neutralized.
   - ○ **Components:** Malware analysis and removal, patching vulnerabilities, cleaning infected systems, and verifying the eradication.

5. **Recovery:**
   - ○ **Description:** Restoring affected systems and services to normal operations while ensuring that the threat has been eradicated and the environment is secure.
   - ○ **Components:** Restoring from backups, rebuilding systems, conducting post-incident testing, and verifying the integrity of restored systems.

6. **Lessons Learned:**
   - ○ **Description:** Reviewing the incident response process to identify areas for improvement and prevent future incidents. This stage involves documenting findings and updating the incident response plan.
   - ○ **Components:** Post-incident review, root cause analysis, documentation, and updates to the incident response plan.

Principles of Digital Forensics

Digital forensics involves the investigation and analysis of digital evidence to determine the root cause, impact, and scope of a security incident. Key principles of digital forensics include:

1. **Preservation:**
   - **Description:** Preserving digital evidence in its original state to ensure its integrity and admissibility in legal proceedings.
   - **Practices:** Create forensic images of affected systems, use write-blockers to prevent data modification, and maintain a chain of custody.

2. **Acquisition:**
   - **Description:** Acquiring digital evidence in a forensically sound manner, ensuring that the evidence is collected without altering or contaminating it.
   - **Practices:** Use standardized forensic tools and procedures, document the acquisition process, and verify the integrity of collected evidence.

3. **Analysis:**
   - **Description:** Analyzing digital evidence to identify relevant information, reconstruct events, and determine the root cause of the incident.
   - **Practices:** Conduct timeline analysis, examine file systems and metadata, perform memory analysis, and analyze network traffic.

4. **Documentation:**
   - **Description:** Documenting all steps taken during the forensic investigation to ensure transparency and reproducibility. Detailed documentation is essential for legal proceedings and post-incident reviews.
   - **Practices:** Maintain detailed notes, create

forensic reports, document findings, and record the tools and techniques used.

5. **Presentation:**

  ◦ **Description:** Presenting the findings of the forensic investigation in a clear and concise manner, suitable for legal proceedings, management reviews, and other stakeholders.

  ◦ **Practices:** Create comprehensive forensic reports, prepare visual aids (e.g., timelines, diagrams), and provide expert testimony if required.

Forensic Tools and Techniques

Digital forensics involves the use of specialized tools and techniques to collect, analyze, and interpret digital evidence. Common forensic tools and techniques include:

1. **Forensic Imaging:**

  ◦ **Description:** Creating an exact copy (image) of a digital storage device for analysis. Forensic images preserve the original data and allow investigators to work on a copy.

  ◦ **Tools:** FTK Imager, EnCase, dd (Linux command).

2. **File System Analysis:**

  ◦ **Description:** Analyzing the file system to identify relevant files, recover deleted data, and examine metadata. This helps reconstruct events and identify malicious activities.

  ◦ **Tools:** Autopsy, Sleuth Kit, X-Ways Forensics.

3. **Memory Analysis:**

  ◦ **Description:** Analyzing the contents of a computer's memory (RAM) to identify running processes, open network connections, and artifacts left by malware.

- **Tools:** Volatility, Redline, Rekall.

4. **Network Forensics:**

- **Description:** Analyzing network traffic to identify suspicious activities, detect intrusions, and reconstruct network-based attacks.
- **Tools:** Wireshark, NetworkMiner, tcpdump.

5. **Log Analysis:**

- **Description:** Analyzing log files from various sources (e.g., system logs, application logs, firewall logs) to identify anomalies, trace activities, and correlate events.
- **Tools:** Logstash, Splunk, Graylog.

Legal and Ethical Considerations in Forensics

Digital forensics must be conducted within the boundaries of the law and ethical guidelines. Key legal and ethical considerations include:

1. **Legal Authorization:**

- Obtain proper authorization before conducting forensic investigations to ensure compliance with legal requirements and organizational policies.

2. **Preserving Evidence Integrity:**

- Ensure the integrity of digital evidence by following standardized procedures, maintaining a chain of custody, and using write-blockers to prevent data modification.

3. **Confidentiality:**

- Maintain the confidentiality of sensitive information discovered during the forensic investigation. Limit access to authorized personnel and protect data from unauthorized disclosure.

4. **Ethical Conduct:**

   - Adhere to ethical guidelines and industry standards to ensure professionalism, integrity, and accountability in forensic investigations.

Conclusion

Incident response and forensics are essential components of a robust cybersecurity strategy. By understanding the principles and processes of incident response, leveraging forensic tools and techniques, and adhering to legal and ethical guidelines, organizations can effectively manage and mitigate security incidents. This chapter provides a comprehensive overview of incident response and forensics, offering valuable insights for cybersecurity professionals and organizations seeking to enhance their security posture. As the cybersecurity landscape continues to evolve, the importance of incident response and forensics in safeguarding digital assets cannot be overstated.

CHAPTER 18:
SECURING EMERGING TECHNOLOGIES

Introduction

As technology continues to evolve, emerging technologies are becoming integral to business operations and daily life. While these technologies offer significant benefits and opportunities, they also present new security challenges and vulnerabilities. This chapter explores the security considerations and best practices for securing emerging technologies, including the Internet of Things (IoT), 5G, artificial intelligence (AI), and blockchain.

Securing Internet of Things (IoT)

The Internet of Things (IoT) encompasses a vast network of interconnected devices that collect, transmit, and analyze data. Securing IoT devices is crucial to protect sensitive information, prevent unauthorized access, and ensure the reliability of IoT systems. Key security considerations and best practices for IoT include:

1. **Device Authentication and Authorization:**
   - **Description:** Implement strong authentication and authorization mechanisms to ensure that only legitimate devices and users can access the IoT network.
   - **Practices:** Use device certificates, implement

mutual authentication, and enforce role-based access control (RBAC).

2. **Data Encryption:**
   - **Description:** Encrypt data at rest and in transit to protect it from eavesdropping and tampering. Use strong encryption algorithms and secure key management practices.
   - **Practices:** Enable end-to-end encryption, use secure communication protocols (e.g., TLS/ SSL), and implement key rotation policies.

3. **Firmware and Software Updates:**
   - **Description:** Ensure that IoT devices receive regular firmware and software updates to address security vulnerabilities and improve functionality.
   - **Practices:** Implement secure update mechanisms, verify the authenticity of updates, and enable automatic updates where possible.

4. **Network Segmentation:**
   - **Description:** Segment the IoT network from other critical networks to limit the impact of potential security breaches and contain threats.
   - **Practices:** Use virtual LANs (VLANs), firewalls, and network access control (NAC) to enforce segmentation.

5. **Monitoring and Incident Response:**
   - **Description:** Continuously monitor IoT devices and networks for security threats and anomalies. Establish an incident response plan to address security incidents promptly.
   - **Practices:** Use intrusion detection systems

(IDS), implement logging and monitoring solutions, and conduct regular security assessments.

Securing 5G Networks

The rollout of 5G networks introduces new security challenges and opportunities due to increased connectivity, lower latency, and higher data transfer rates. Securing 5G networks is essential to protect sensitive data and ensure the reliability of communication services. Key security considerations and best practices for 5G include:

1. **Enhanced Encryption:**
   - **Description:** Utilize advanced encryption algorithms to protect data transmitted over 5G networks. Ensure that encryption is implemented end-to-end.
   - **Practices:** Use AES-256 encryption, implement secure key exchange protocols, and enable encryption for voice, data, and signaling.

2. **Network Slicing Security:**
   - **Description:** Network slicing allows the creation of virtual networks within a 5G network, each with its own security policies and configurations. Ensure that each slice is securely isolated and protected.
   - **Practices:** Implement access controls for each slice, use software-defined networking (SDN) for dynamic segmentation, and enforce security policies based on the sensitivity of data.

3. **Edge Computing Security:**
   - **Description:** 5G networks enable edge computing, where data processing occurs closer to the source. Ensure that edge

computing environments are secure to protect against potential threats.

- ◦ **Practices:** Use secure containers and virtualization, implement access controls, and encrypt data at the edge.

4. **Supply Chain Security:**
   - ◦ **Description:** Secure the 5G supply chain to prevent tampering and ensure the integrity of network components and software.
   - ◦ **Practices:** Conduct thorough vetting of suppliers, use secure boot and firmware validation, and implement hardware-based security measures.

5. **Threat Detection and Response:**
   - ◦ **Description:** Continuously monitor 5G networks for security threats and respond to incidents promptly. Use AI and machine learning to enhance threat detection capabilities.
   - ◦ **Practices:** Implement advanced threat detection systems, use network traffic analysis, and conduct regular penetration testing and security audits.

Securing Artificial Intelligence (AI)

Artificial intelligence (AI) technologies offer significant advantages in various fields, including cybersecurity, healthcare, and finance. However, securing AI systems is essential to protect against adversarial attacks and ensure the integrity and reliability of AI models. Key security considerations and best practices for AI include:

1. **Adversarial Robustness:**
   - ◦ **Description:** Ensure that AI models are robust against adversarial attacks, where malicious

inputs are crafted to deceive the model and produce incorrect outputs.

- **Practices:** Use adversarial training, implement input validation, and employ defensive distillation techniques.

2. **Data Privacy and Integrity:**

- **Description:** Protect the privacy and integrity of data used to train AI models to prevent data poisoning and unauthorized access.
- **Practices:** Use differential privacy techniques, implement access controls for training data, and monitor data usage.

3. **Model Explainability:**

- **Description:** Ensure that AI models are interpretable and explainable to allow for better understanding and verification of their decision-making processes.
- **Practices:** Use explainable AI techniques, provide transparency reports, and involve domain experts in model validation.

4. **Secure Deployment:**

- **Description:** Securely deploy AI models to prevent unauthorized access and tampering. Use secure environments for model inference and updates.
- **Practices:** Implement access controls, use containerization and sandboxing, and verify the integrity of deployed models.

5. **Ethical Considerations:**

- **Description:** Ensure that AI systems are designed and deployed ethically, considering potential biases and ensuring fairness and accountability.

- **Practices:** Conduct ethical reviews, implement fairness metrics, and involve diverse teams in the development and evaluation of AI models.

Securing Blockchain Technology

Blockchain technology offers significant benefits for secure and transparent transactions, but it also presents unique security challenges. Securing blockchain implementations is crucial to protect against attacks and ensure the integrity of the blockchain. Key security considerations and best practices for blockchain include:

1. **Consensus Mechanisms:**
   - **Description:** Implement secure consensus mechanisms to ensure the integrity and reliability of the blockchain. Protect against attacks such as 51% attacks and double-spending.
   - **Practices:** Use proof-of-work (PoW), proof-of-stake (PoS), or other consensus mechanisms with strong security guarantees.

2. **Smart Contract Security:**
   - **Description:** Ensure that smart contracts are secure and free from vulnerabilities that could be exploited by attackers.
   - **Practices:** Conduct thorough code reviews, use formal verification, and implement secure coding practices.

3. **Key Management:**
   - **Description:** Protect private keys used for signing transactions to prevent unauthorized access and misuse.
   - **Practices:** Use hardware security modules (HSMs), implement multi-signature schemes,

and enforce secure key storage and backup.

4. **Network Security:**

   ◦ **Description:** Secure the blockchain network to prevent unauthorized access, DDoS attacks, and other network-based threats.

   ◦ **Practices:** Implement network segmentation, use encryption for network communication, and monitor network traffic for anomalies.

5. **Governance and Compliance:**

   ◦ **Description:** Establish governance frameworks and ensure compliance with relevant regulations and standards to maintain the security and integrity of the blockchain.

   ◦ **Practices:** Define roles and responsibilities, implement access controls, and conduct regular security audits and assessments.

Conclusion

Securing emerging technologies is essential to protect sensitive data, prevent unauthorized access, and ensure the reliability and integrity of digital systems. By understanding the unique security challenges and implementing best practices for IoT, 5G, AI, and blockchain, organizations can enhance their cybersecurity posture and leverage the benefits of these technologies safely and effectively. This chapter provides a comprehensive overview of securing emerging technologies, offering valuable insights for cybersecurity professionals and organizations seeking to stay ahead of evolving threats and vulnerabilities. As technology continues to advance, the importance of proactive security measures in safeguarding digital assets cannot be overstated.

CHAPTER 19: CYBERSECURITY FOR REMOTE WORK

Introduction

The shift to remote work has transformed the modern workplace, offering employees flexibility and convenience. However, this transition also introduces new cybersecurity challenges and risks. As organizations increasingly adopt remote work models, ensuring the security of remote work environments becomes paramount. This chapter explores the key cybersecurity considerations and best practices for securing remote work, helping organizations protect sensitive data and maintain business continuity.

Key Cybersecurity Risks in Remote Work

Remote work environments present several unique cybersecurity risks that organizations must address to protect their digital assets. Common risks include:

1. **Phishing Attacks:**
   - **Description:** Phishing attacks involve sending fraudulent emails or messages to trick individuals into disclosing sensitive information or downloading malicious attachments. Remote workers are often targeted due to the lack of direct oversight and increased reliance on digital communication.

- **Impact:** Compromised credentials, unauthorized access to corporate networks, data breaches.

2. **Unsecured Wi-Fi Networks:**

   - **Description:** Remote workers may connect to unsecured Wi-Fi networks, such as public Wi-Fi or home networks with weak security configurations. These networks can be easily compromised by attackers.

   - **Impact:** Eavesdropping on sensitive communications, interception of data, network intrusions.

3. **Inadequate Endpoint Security:**

   - **Description:** Remote work often involves using personal devices or company-issued laptops outside the corporate network. Inadequate endpoint security can leave these devices vulnerable to malware, ransomware, and other threats.

   - **Impact:** Device compromise, data loss, spread of malware to corporate networks.

4. **Insider Threats:**

   - **Description:** Insider threats involve employees or contractors who misuse their access privileges to harm the organization. Remote work can make it challenging to monitor and detect insider threats.

   - **Impact:** Data theft, intellectual property loss, sabotage.

5. **Lack of Security Awareness:**

   - **Description:** Remote workers may lack the necessary cybersecurity awareness and training to identify and respond to security threats. This can lead to risky behaviors and increased susceptibility to attacks.

- **Impact:** Increased risk of falling victim to phishing, social engineering, and other cyber threats.

Best Practices for Securing Remote Work

To mitigate the cybersecurity risks associated with remote work, organizations should implement a comprehensive set of best practices. Key best practices include:

1. **Implement Strong Authentication:**
   - **Description:** Use strong authentication mechanisms to verify the identity of remote workers and secure access to corporate resources.
   - **Practices:** Implement multi-factor authentication (MFA), use strong and unique passwords, and enforce regular password changes.

2. **Secure Remote Access:**
   - **Description:** Ensure that remote access to corporate networks and resources is secure to prevent unauthorized access and data breaches.
   - **Practices:** Use virtual private networks (VPNs), implement secure remote desktop solutions, and configure firewalls and access controls.

3. **Enhance Endpoint Security:**
   - **Description:** Protect remote work devices from malware, ransomware, and other threats by implementing robust endpoint security measures.
   - **Practices:** Use endpoint protection software,

enable encryption for data at rest, enforce security policies for devices, and ensure regular software updates and patches.

4. **Conduct Security Awareness Training:**
   - **Description:** Provide regular security awareness training to remote workers to educate them about common cybersecurity threats and best practices.
   - **Practices:** Conduct phishing simulation exercises, offer online training modules, and share security tips and guidelines.

5. **Secure Communication Channels:**
   - **Description:** Use secure communication channels to protect sensitive information transmitted between remote workers and the corporate network.
   - **Practices:** Use encrypted communication tools (e.g., secure email, instant messaging), enforce secure file-sharing practices, and avoid using public or unsecured communication platforms.

6. **Monitor and Respond to Security Incidents:**
   - **Description:** Continuously monitor remote work environments for security threats and respond promptly to security incidents to minimize impact.
   - **Practices:** Use security information and event management (SIEM) solutions, implement real-time monitoring and alerting, and establish an incident response plan.

Securing Remote Access Solutions

Remote access solutions, such as VPNs and remote desktop services, are essential for enabling remote work. Securing these solutions is crucial to protect against unauthorized access and ensure the confidentiality and integrity of data. Key considerations for securing remote access solutions include:

1. **Virtual Private Networks (VPNs):**
   - **Description:** VPNs create a secure and encrypted connection between remote workers and the corporate network. They protect data transmitted over the internet and provide a secure channel for remote access.
   - **Practices:** Use strong encryption protocols (e.g., AES-256), implement multi-factor authentication (MFA) for VPN access, enforce strict access controls, and regularly update VPN software.

2. **Remote Desktop Services:**
   - **Description:** Remote desktop services allow remote workers to access their office desktops or servers from any location. Securing these services is essential to prevent unauthorized access and ensure data protection.
   - **Practices:** Use secure remote desktop protocols (e.g., RDP, VNC) with encryption, configure firewalls to restrict remote desktop access, implement account lockout policies, and enable logging and monitoring.

3. **Zero Trust Architecture:**
   - **Description:** Zero Trust architecture is a security model that assumes no implicit trust within the network and requires continuous verification of users and devices. It enhances security by enforcing strict access controls and monitoring all activities.
   - **Practices:** Implement micro-segmentation, use identity and access management (IAM)

solutions, enforce least privilege access, and continuously monitor and assess security policies.

Protecting Data in Remote Work Environments

Protecting sensitive data is a critical aspect of securing remote work environments. Organizations must implement measures to ensure the confidentiality, integrity, and availability of data. Key best practices for data protection include:

1. **Data Encryption:**
   - **Description:** Encrypt sensitive data at rest and in transit to protect it from unauthorized access and tampering.
   - **Practices:** Use strong encryption algorithms (e.g., AES-256), encrypt data stored on remote work devices, and enable encryption for all communication channels.

2. **Data Loss Prevention (DLP):**
   - **Description:** Implement data loss prevention (DLP) solutions to monitor and protect sensitive data from being accidentally or maliciously leaked.
   - **Practices:** Use DLP tools to monitor data transfers, enforce policies for handling sensitive data, and block unauthorized access to data.

3. **Secure Data Storage:**
   - **Description:** Ensure that data stored on remote work devices and cloud storage solutions is secure and protected from unauthorized access.
   - **Practices:** Use secure cloud storage services with encryption, implement access controls for cloud storage, and regularly back up data

to prevent data loss.

4. **Access Controls:**
   - **Description:** Implement access controls to ensure that only authorized users can access sensitive data and resources.
   - **Practices:** Use role-based access control (RBAC), enforce least privilege access, and regularly review and update access permissions.

Compliance and Regulatory Considerations

Organizations must ensure that remote work environments comply with relevant regulations and industry standards to protect sensitive data and maintain legal and regulatory compliance. Key considerations include:

1. **General Data Protection Regulation (GDPR):**
   - **Description:** GDPR sets standards for data protection and privacy for individuals within the European Union (EU). Organizations must comply with GDPR requirements when processing personal data of EU residents.
   - **Practices:** Implement data protection measures, obtain consent for data processing, provide data access and deletion rights, and report data breaches within 72 hours.

2. **Health Insurance Portability and Accountability Act (HIPAA):**
   - **Description:** HIPAA sets standards for protecting the privacy and security of health information in the United States. Organizations handling protected health information (PHI) must comply with HIPAA requirements.
   - **Practices:** Implement administrative,

physical, and technical safeguards, ensure data confidentiality and integrity, conduct regular risk assessments, and report security incidents.

3. **Payment Card Industry Data Security Standard (PCI DSS):**

   ◦ **Description:** PCI DSS is a set of security standards for organizations handling credit card transactions. It aims to protect cardholder data and prevent data breaches.

   ◦ **Practices:** Implement strong access controls, encrypt cardholder data, maintain secure systems and applications, and conduct regular security testing and monitoring.

Conclusion

Securing remote work environments is essential to protect sensitive data, prevent unauthorized access, and ensure business continuity. By understanding the key cybersecurity risks and implementing best practices for authentication, remote access, endpoint security, data protection, and compliance, organizations can create a secure and resilient remote work infrastructure. This chapter provides a comprehensive overview of cybersecurity considerations for remote work, offering valuable insights for organizations and cybersecurity professionals seeking to enhance their security posture in the remote work era. As remote work continues to evolve, the importance of proactive security measures in safeguarding digital assets and maintaining business operations cannot be overstated.

CHAPTER 20:
THE FUTURE OF
CYBERSECURITY

Introduction

The field of cybersecurity is constantly evolving, driven by advancements in technology, changes in the threat landscape, and increasing awareness of the importance of protecting digital assets. As we look to the future, it is essential to understand the emerging trends, challenges, and opportunities that will shape the cybersecurity landscape. This chapter explores the future of cybersecurity, highlighting key trends, potential threats, and strategies for staying ahead in this dynamic field.

Key Trends in Cybersecurity

Several key trends are expected to influence the future of cybersecurity. Understanding these trends can help organizations and individuals prepare for the challenges and opportunities that lie ahead. Key trends include:

1. **Artificial Intelligence (AI) and Machine Learning (ML):**
   - **Description:** AI and ML technologies are becoming increasingly integral to cybersecurity, providing advanced tools for threat detection, analysis, and response.
   - **Impact:** Enhanced ability to identify and

mitigate threats in real-time, improved accuracy in detecting anomalies, and reduced reliance on manual processes.

2. **Zero Trust Security Model:**

    ◦ **Description:** The Zero Trust security model assumes no implicit trust within the network and requires continuous verification of users and devices. This approach minimizes the attack surface and enhances security.

    ◦ **Impact:** Improved access control, reduced risk of lateral movement by attackers, and enhanced protection of critical assets.

3. **Cloud Security:**

    ◦ **Description:** As organizations continue to migrate to the cloud, securing cloud environments becomes paramount. Cloud security involves protecting data, applications, and infrastructure hosted in cloud services.

    ◦ **Impact:** Increased focus on cloud-native security solutions, greater emphasis on data encryption and access controls, and improved visibility into cloud activities.

4. **Quantum Computing:**

    ◦ **Description:** Quantum computing has the potential to revolutionize cybersecurity by breaking traditional encryption algorithms. However, it also offers opportunities for developing quantum-resistant cryptography and enhancing security.

    ◦ **Impact:** Need for quantum-resistant cryptographic algorithms, increased investment in quantum-safe security solutions, and potential for advanced threat detection capabilities.

5. **IoT Security:**
   - **Description:** The proliferation of Internet of Things (IoT) devices introduces new security challenges. Securing IoT environments is essential to protect sensitive data and ensure the reliability of connected systems.
   - **Impact:** Greater emphasis on device authentication, data encryption, and secure firmware updates, as well as the development of IoT-specific security frameworks.

6. **Regulatory Compliance:**
   - **Description:** The evolving regulatory landscape requires organizations to comply with various data protection and cybersecurity regulations. Compliance with these regulations is essential to avoid legal penalties and protect sensitive data.
   - **Impact:** Increased focus on data privacy and protection, greater accountability for data breaches, and the need for continuous monitoring and auditing.

Potential Future Threats

As the cybersecurity landscape evolves, new threats and attack vectors are likely to emerge. Understanding potential future threats can help organizations and individuals proactively address security challenges. Potential future threats include:

1. **Advanced Persistent Threats (APTs):**
   - **Description:** APTs are sophisticated, long-term attacks aimed at stealing sensitive information or disrupting operations. They often involve multiple attack vectors and tactics to evade detection.

- **Impact:** Increased risk of data breaches, intellectual property theft, and disruption of critical services.

2. **Ransomware Evolution:**

   - **Description:** Ransomware attacks are becoming more targeted and sophisticated, with attackers demanding higher ransoms and employing new tactics to pressure victims.
   - **Impact:** Significant financial losses, disruption of business operations, and potential damage to reputation.

3. **Supply Chain Attacks:**

   - **Description:** Supply chain attacks target third-party vendors and service providers to compromise the security of organizations that rely on them. These attacks can introduce vulnerabilities into the supply chain.
   - **Impact:** Increased risk of data breaches, unauthorized access, and disruption of operations across multiple organizations.

4. **IoT Botnets:**

   - **Description:** IoT botnets are networks of compromised IoT devices used to launch distributed denial-of-service (DDoS) attacks and other malicious activities.
   - **Impact:** Increased frequency and scale of DDoS attacks, disruption of critical services, and potential for large-scale cyber incidents.

5. **Deepfakes and AI-Driven Attacks:**

   - **Description:** Deepfakes involve using AI to create realistic fake images, videos, or audio recordings. AI-driven attacks use machine learning algorithms to automate and enhance cyberattacks.

- ◦ **Impact:** Increased risk of misinformation, social engineering attacks, and manipulation of public opinion.

Strategies for Staying Ahead

To stay ahead in the evolving cybersecurity landscape, organizations and individuals must adopt proactive strategies and continuously improve their security posture. Key strategies for staying ahead include:

1. **Continuous Learning and Training:**

   - ◦ **Description:** Stay informed about the latest cybersecurity trends, threats, and best practices through continuous learning and training. Regularly update skills and knowledge to stay current.
   - ◦ **Practices:** Attend industry conferences, participate in training programs, obtain relevant certifications, and engage with cybersecurity communities.

2. **Implementing Advanced Security Technologies:**

   - ◦ **Description:** Leverage advanced security technologies, such as AI and ML, to enhance threat detection, analysis, and response capabilities.
   - ◦ **Practices:** Invest in AI-powered security solutions, implement automated threat detection and response, and use predictive analytics to anticipate and mitigate threats.

3. **Adopting a Zero Trust Approach:**

   - ◦ **Description:** Implement a Zero Trust security model to enhance access controls and minimize the attack surface. Continuously verify the identity of users and devices.

- **Practices:** Use multi-factor authentication (MFA), implement micro-segmentation, enforce least privilege access, and monitor all network activities.

4. **Enhancing Threat Intelligence:**

- **Description:** Utilize threat intelligence to stay informed about emerging threats and attack vectors. Integrate threat intelligence into security operations to improve threat detection and response.
- **Practices:** Subscribe to threat intelligence feeds, participate in information-sharing networks, and use threat intelligence platforms.

5. **Strengthening Incident Response Capabilities:**

- **Description:** Develop and maintain robust incident response capabilities to effectively manage and mitigate security incidents. Ensure that incident response plans are regularly tested and updated.
- **Practices:** Establish an incident response team (IRT), conduct regular incident response drills, use incident response automation, and perform post-incident reviews.

6. **Fostering a Security-First Culture:**

- **Description:** Promote a security-first culture within the organization by emphasizing the importance of cybersecurity and encouraging best practices among employees.
- **Practices:** Provide regular security awareness training, implement security policies and guidelines, encourage reporting of security incidents, and recognize and reward good

security practices.

Conclusion

The future of cybersecurity is shaped by emerging technologies, evolving threats, and increasing regulatory requirements. By understanding key trends, potential future threats, and adopting proactive strategies, organizations and individuals can enhance their cybersecurity posture and stay ahead in this dynamic field. This chapter provides a comprehensive overview of the future of cybersecurity, offering valuable insights for cybersecurity professionals and organizations seeking to navigate the challenges and opportunities that lie ahead. As we look to the future, the importance of continuous learning, innovation, and collaboration in safeguarding digital assets and ensuring a secure digital world cannot be overstated.

CHAPTER 21: BUILDING A CYBERSECURITY CULTURE

Introduction

Creating a strong cybersecurity culture is essential for protecting an organization's digital assets, ensuring compliance with regulatory requirements, and fostering a secure work environment. A cybersecurity culture involves instilling security awareness, best practices, and behaviors across all levels of the organization. This chapter explores the importance of building a cybersecurity culture, key components of a strong cybersecurity culture, and strategies for fostering a security-first mindset among employees.

Importance of a Cybersecurity Culture

A robust cybersecurity culture is vital for several reasons:

1. **Enhanced Security Posture:**
   - **Description:** A strong cybersecurity culture ensures that employees are aware of security threats and take proactive measures to protect the organization's digital assets.
   - **Benefits:** Reduced risk of security breaches, improved incident response capabilities, and enhanced overall security posture.

2. **Regulatory Compliance:**
   - **Description:** Compliance with data protection and cybersecurity regulations often requires organizations to implement security awareness programs and best practices.
   - **Benefits:** Avoidance of legal penalties, protection of sensitive data, and adherence to industry standards.

3. **Employee Empowerment:**
   - **Description:** A cybersecurity culture empowers employees to take responsibility for their actions and contribute to the organization's security efforts.
   - **Benefits:** Increased security awareness, proactive identification of security threats, and a sense of ownership among employees.

4. **Reputation Protection:**
   - **Description:** A strong cybersecurity culture helps protect the organization's reputation by preventing data breaches and ensuring the confidentiality, integrity, and availability of data.
   - **Benefits:** Maintained trust and confidence among customers, partners, and stakeholders.

Key Components of a Strong Cybersecurity Culture

Building a strong cybersecurity culture involves several key components:

1. **Leadership and Governance:**
   - **Description:** Senior leadership must demonstrate a commitment to cybersecurity and provide the necessary resources and support for security initiatives.

- **Practices:** Establish a cybersecurity governance framework, appoint a Chief Information Security Officer (CISO), and ensure leadership involvement in security decision-making.

2. **Security Awareness and Training:**
   - **Description:** Regular security awareness and training programs educate employees about cybersecurity threats and best practices.
   - **Practices:** Conduct mandatory security training sessions, provide ongoing education through workshops and webinars, and use engaging training materials (e.g., videos, quizzes).

3. **Clear Policies and Procedures:**
   - **Description:** Well-defined cybersecurity policies and procedures provide employees with guidelines for acceptable behavior and actions.
   - **Practices:** Develop and communicate security policies (e.g., password policies, data handling procedures), ensure policies are easily accessible, and conduct regular policy reviews.

4. **Incident Reporting and Response:**
   - **Description:** Encourage employees to report security incidents and establish a clear process for responding to and managing incidents.
   - **Practices:** Implement an incident reporting system, provide clear guidelines for reporting incidents, and establish an incident response team (IRT) with defined roles and responsibilities.

5. **Regular Communication and Engagement:**
   ○ **Description:** Regular communication and engagement with employees help reinforce the importance of cybersecurity and keep them informed about security updates and initiatives.
   ○ **Practices:** Use internal communication channels (e.g., emails, newsletters, intranet) to share security tips and updates, organize security-themed events, and recognize employees for good security practices.

Strategies for Fostering a Cybersecurity Mindset

To foster a cybersecurity mindset among employees, organizations should implement the following strategies:

1. **Lead by Example:**
   ○ **Description:** Leadership and management should model good cybersecurity behavior and demonstrate their commitment to security.
   ○ **Practices:** Follow security policies and procedures, participate in security training, and actively promote security initiatives.

2. **Incorporate Security into Daily Activities:**
   ○ **Description:** Integrate cybersecurity into employees' daily activities and workflows to make security a natural part of their routine.
   ○ **Practices:** Use secure communication tools, enforce secure coding practices, and ensure that security considerations are part of project planning and decision-making processes.

3. **Recognize and Reward Good Security Practices:**
   ○ **Description:** Recognize and reward

employees who demonstrate good security practices to encourage positive behavior.

- **Practices:** Implement a rewards and recognition program, highlight security champions in internal communications, and provide incentives for reporting security incidents.

4. **Address Security as a Shared Responsibility:**

   - **Description:** Emphasize that cybersecurity is a shared responsibility and that everyone in the organization plays a role in protecting digital assets.

   - **Practices:** Create cross-functional security teams, involve employees in security initiatives, and foster a sense of collective responsibility.

5. **Use Real-World Scenarios:**

   - **Description:** Use real-world scenarios and case studies to illustrate the importance of cybersecurity and the potential impact of security breaches.

   - **Practices:** Incorporate case studies into training sessions, share examples of recent security incidents, and conduct tabletop exercises to simulate security incidents.

6. **Provide Accessible Security Resources:**

   - **Description:** Ensure that employees have access to resources and tools that help them understand and implement good security practices.

   - **Practices:** Create a centralized repository of security resources (e.g., guidelines, training materials), offer security help desks or support channels, and provide easy-to-use security tools.

Measuring and Assessing Cybersecurity Culture

To ensure the effectiveness of cybersecurity culture initiatives, organizations should regularly measure and assess their cybersecurity culture. Key steps include:

1. **Conduct Security Assessments:**
   - **Description:** Conduct regular security assessments to evaluate the organization's security posture and identify areas for improvement.
   - **Practices:** Use security audits, vulnerability assessments, and penetration testing to assess the effectiveness of security controls and practices.

2. **Employee Surveys and Feedback:**
   - **Description:** Collect feedback from employees to understand their perceptions of cybersecurity and identify areas where additional training or resources may be needed.
   - **Practices:** Use anonymous surveys, conduct focus groups, and encourage open feedback channels.

3. **Monitor Security Metrics:**
   - **Description:** Monitor key security metrics to track the progress of cybersecurity initiatives and identify trends or areas of concern.
   - **Practices:** Track metrics such as the number of reported incidents, completion rates of security training, and compliance with security policies.

4. **Perform Regular Reviews:**
   - **Description:** Regularly review and update

cybersecurity policies, procedures, and training programs to ensure they remain relevant and effective.

- **Practices:** Conduct annual policy reviews, update training materials based on emerging threats, and incorporate feedback from security assessments.

Conclusion

Building a strong cybersecurity culture is essential for protecting an organization's digital assets, ensuring compliance with regulatory requirements, and fostering a secure work environment. By implementing best practices for leadership and governance, security awareness and training, clear policies and procedures, incident reporting and response, and regular communication and engagement, organizations can create a culture where cybersecurity is a shared responsibility and an integral part of daily activities. This chapter provides a comprehensive overview of the key components and strategies for building a cybersecurity culture, offering valuable insights for organizations seeking to enhance their security posture and protect against evolving cyber threats. As the cybersecurity landscape continues to evolve, the importance of fostering a strong cybersecurity culture in safeguarding digital assets and ensuring business continuity cannot be overstated.

CHAPTER 22: CYBERSECURITY FOR SMALL AND MEDIUM-SIZED ENTERPRISES (SMES)

Introduction

Small and medium-sized enterprises (SMEs) are the backbone of many economies, contributing significantly to innovation, employment, and economic growth. However, SMEs are often targeted by cybercriminals due to their perceived lack of robust security measures and resources. This chapter explores the unique cybersecurity challenges faced by SMEs, offers best practices for securing their digital assets, and provides guidance on building a resilient cybersecurity framework.

Unique Cybersecurity Challenges for SMEs

SMEs face several unique cybersecurity challenges that can make them vulnerable to cyberattacks. Key challenges include:

1. **Limited Resources:**
   ○ **Description:** SMEs often have limited financial and human resources to dedicate to cybersecurity initiatives, making it challenging to implement comprehensive security measures.

◦ **Impact:** Inadequate security infrastructure, lack of specialized cybersecurity staff, and reliance on basic security tools.

2. **Lack of Awareness:**

   ◦ **Description:** SME owners and employees may lack awareness and understanding of cybersecurity threats and best practices, leading to risky behaviors and practices.

   ◦ **Impact:** Increased susceptibility to phishing attacks, weak password practices, and failure to recognize and respond to security incidents.

3. **Outdated Technology:**

   ◦ **Description:** SMEs may use outdated technology and software that are more vulnerable to cyberattacks due to unpatched security vulnerabilities.

   ◦ **Impact:** Increased risk of malware infections, data breaches, and exploitation of known vulnerabilities.

4. **Third-Party Risks:**

   ◦ **Description:** SMEs often rely on third-party vendors and service providers for various business functions. These third parties can introduce security risks if they are not adequately vetted and secured.

   ◦ **Impact:** Data breaches, unauthorized access, and supply chain attacks.

5. **Compliance Challenges:**

   ◦ **Description:** SMEs may struggle to comply with cybersecurity and data protection regulations due to the complexity and cost of implementing required controls.

       ◦ **Impact:** Legal penalties, reputational damage, and loss of customer trust.

Best Practices for Securing SMEs

To address these challenges and enhance their cybersecurity posture, SMEs should implement a set of best practices tailored to their specific needs and resources. Key best practices include:

1. **Conduct Risk Assessments:**

         ◦ **Description:** Perform regular risk assessments to identify and prioritize cybersecurity risks and vulnerabilities. Understanding the specific threats faced by the organization is essential for implementing effective security measures.

         ◦ **Practices:** Identify critical assets, assess potential threats, evaluate the impact of potential security incidents, and develop a risk management plan.

2. **Implement Basic Security Measures:**

         ◦ **Description:** Start with fundamental security measures that provide a solid foundation for protecting digital assets. Basic security measures are often cost-effective and easy to implement.

         ◦ **Practices:** Use strong passwords and enforce password policies, enable multi-factor authentication (MFA), install antivirus and anti-malware software, and ensure regular software updates and patches.

3. **Secure Network Infrastructure:**

         ◦ **Description:** Protect the organization's network infrastructure to prevent unauthorized access and minimize the risk of cyberattacks.

- **Practices:** Use firewalls to control incoming and outgoing traffic, implement virtual private networks (VPNs) for secure remote access, segment the network to isolate sensitive systems, and configure wireless networks securely.

4. **Provide Security Awareness Training:**

   - **Description:** Educate employees about cybersecurity threats and best practices to reduce the risk of human error and improve overall security awareness.

   - **Practices:** Conduct regular security training sessions, provide phishing simulation exercises, share security tips and guidelines, and encourage employees to report suspicious activities.

5. **Develop an Incident Response Plan:**

   - **Description:** Establish an incident response plan to effectively manage and mitigate security incidents. A well-defined plan ensures a coordinated and timely response to cyber threats.

   - **Practices:** Define roles and responsibilities, establish communication protocols, conduct incident response drills, and document incident response procedures.

6. **Backup Critical Data:**

   - **Description:** Regularly backup critical data to protect against data loss due to cyberattacks, hardware failures, or other disasters. Ensure that backups are stored securely and can be easily restored.

   - **Practices:** Implement automated backup solutions, store backups in multiple locations (e.g., cloud, offsite storage), test backup and restore processes regularly, and encrypt backup data.

7. **Vet Third-Party Vendors:**
    ◦ **Description:** Assess the security practices of third-party vendors and service providers to ensure they meet the organization's cybersecurity standards.
    ◦ **Practices:** Conduct due diligence, require security assessments and certifications, include security requirements in contracts, and monitor third-party activities for compliance.

Building a Cybersecurity Framework for SMEs

Building a cybersecurity framework provides a structured approach to managing cybersecurity risks and implementing security measures. Key steps to building a cybersecurity framework for SMEs include:

1. **Define Security Policies:**
    ◦ **Description:** Develop and document security policies that outline the organization's approach to cybersecurity and provide guidelines for employees and stakeholders.
    ◦ **Components:** Data protection policies, access control policies, incident response policies, acceptable use policies, and third-party security policies.

2. **Establish Governance:**
    ◦ **Description:** Create a governance structure to oversee and manage the organization's cybersecurity initiatives. Governance ensures accountability and alignment with business objectives.

- ○ **Components:** Appoint a cybersecurity leader (e.g., IT manager or CISO), form a cybersecurity committee, establish roles and responsibilities, and conduct regular governance meetings.

3. **Implement Security Controls:**
   - ○ **Description:** Implement security controls based on the risk assessment and security policies. Security controls protect critical assets and mitigate identified risks.
   - ○ **Components:** Technical controls (e.g., firewalls, encryption, access controls), administrative controls (e.g., training, policies, procedures), and physical controls (e.g., security locks, surveillance).

4. **Monitor and Assess:**
   - ○ **Description:** Continuously monitor the organization's security posture and assess the effectiveness of implemented security measures. Monitoring helps identify potential threats and areas for improvement.
   - ○ **Components:** Use security information and event management (SIEM) systems, conduct regular vulnerability assessments and penetration testing, and review security metrics and reports.

5. **Review and Improve:**
   - ○ **Description:** Regularly review and update the cybersecurity framework to adapt to changing threats and business needs. Continuous improvement ensures that the organization remains resilient to cyber threats.
   - ○ **Components:** Conduct annual reviews of

security policies and controls, incorporate feedback from security assessments and incident response, and stay informed about emerging threats and best practices.

Accessing Cybersecurity Resources for SMEs

SMEs can leverage various resources and support to enhance their cybersecurity efforts. Key resources include:

1. **Government and Industry Initiatives:**
   - **Description:** Many governments and industry organizations offer cybersecurity resources, guidelines, and support for SMEs.
   - **Examples:** National Cyber Security Centre (NCSC) guidance, Small Business Administration (SBA) cybersecurity resources, industry-specific cybersecurity frameworks (e.g., PCI DSS for payment card industry).

2. **Cybersecurity Frameworks and Standards:**
   - **Description:** Adopting recognized cybersecurity frameworks and standards provides a structured approach to implementing security measures and achieving compliance.
   - **Examples:** NIST Cybersecurity Framework, ISO/IEC 27001, CIS Controls.

3. **Security Vendors and Service Providers:**
   - **Description:** Partnering with reputable security vendors and service providers can help SMEs access advanced security solutions and expertise.
   - **Examples:** Managed security service providers (MSSPs), cybersecurity consulting firms, security software vendors.

4. **Training and Certification Programs:**
   - **Description:** Participating in cybersecurity training and certification programs helps SMEs build internal expertise and stay informed about the latest threats and best practices.
   - **Examples:** CompTIA Security+, Certified Information Systems Security Professional (CISSP), Certified Ethical Hacker (CEH), online training platforms (e.g., Coursera, Udemy).

Conclusion

SMEs face unique cybersecurity challenges that require tailored strategies and best practices to protect their digital assets and ensure business continuity. By conducting risk assessments, implementing basic security measures, providing security awareness training, developing incident response plans, and leveraging available resources, SMEs can build a resilient cybersecurity framework. This chapter provides valuable insights and practical guidance for SMEs seeking to enhance their cybersecurity posture and protect against evolving cyber threats. As the cybersecurity landscape continues to evolve, the importance of proactive security measures and a strong cybersecurity culture in safeguarding digital assets cannot be overstated.

CHAPTER 23: CYBERSECURITY FOR CRITICAL INFRASTRUCTURE

Introduction

Critical infrastructure encompasses the essential systems and assets that support the functioning of a society, including energy, water, transportation, healthcare, and communications. The security of these systems is vital to national security, public safety, and economic stability. As cyber threats targeting critical infrastructure continue to evolve, ensuring the resilience and protection of these assets is paramount. This chapter explores the unique cybersecurity challenges faced by critical infrastructure, best practices for securing these systems, and strategies for enhancing their resilience.

Unique Cybersecurity Challenges for Critical Infrastructure

Critical infrastructure systems face several unique cybersecurity challenges that require specialized approaches and solutions. Key challenges include:

1. **Legacy Systems:**
   - **Description:** Many critical infrastructure systems rely on legacy technologies and software that are no longer supported or updated. These systems may have inherent

vulnerabilities that can be exploited by cyber attackers.

- ◦ **Impact:** Increased risk of cyberattacks, difficulty in implementing modern security measures, and potential for significant disruptions.

2. **Interconnected Systems:**

- ◦ **Description:** Critical infrastructure systems are highly interconnected and interdependent, meaning that a cyberattack on one system can have cascading effects on others.

- ◦ **Impact:** Broader impact of cyberattacks, potential for widespread disruptions, and challenges in isolating and containing incidents.

3. **Operational Technology (OT) and Information Technology (IT) Convergence:**

- ◦ **Description:** The convergence of OT and IT systems introduces new vulnerabilities, as OT systems, traditionally isolated from the internet, are now connected to IT networks.

- ◦ **Impact:** Increased attack surface, potential for remote exploitation of OT systems, and challenges in securing complex, hybrid environments.

4. **Sophisticated Threat Actors:**

- ◦ **Description:** Critical infrastructure systems are often targeted by sophisticated threat actors, including nation-state adversaries, organized crime groups, and hacktivists, who employ advanced tactics and techniques.

- ◦ **Impact:** Increased likelihood of targeted attacks, potential for prolonged and stealthy intrusions, and higher risk of disruptive or destructive cyber activities.

5. **Regulatory Compliance:**

    ◦ **Description:** Critical infrastructure operators must comply with a complex web of regulations and standards designed to ensure the security and resilience of these systems.

    ◦ **Impact:** Resource-intensive compliance efforts, need for continuous monitoring and reporting, and challenges in keeping up with evolving regulatory requirements.

Best Practices for Securing Critical Infrastructure

To address these challenges and enhance the cybersecurity of critical infrastructure, operators should implement a comprehensive set of best practices. Key best practices include:

1. **Risk Assessment and Management:**

    ◦ **Description:** Conduct regular risk assessments to identify and prioritize cybersecurity risks and vulnerabilities. Develop and implement risk management strategies to mitigate identified risks.

    ◦ **Practices:** Identify critical assets and potential threats, assess the impact of potential security incidents, and implement risk mitigation measures.

2. **Segmentation and Isolation:**

    ◦ **Description:** Implement network segmentation and isolation to limit the impact of cyberattacks and prevent lateral movement within critical infrastructure systems.

    ◦ **Practices:** Use firewalls, virtual LANs (VLANs), and demilitarized zones (DMZs) to segment networks, and isolate OT systems from IT networks and the internet.

3. **Access Control and Authentication:**
   - **Description:** Enforce strict access control and authentication mechanisms to ensure that only authorized personnel can access critical infrastructure systems.
   - **Practices:** Implement multi-factor authentication (MFA), use role-based access control (RBAC), enforce least privilege access, and regularly review access permissions.

4. **Continuous Monitoring and Detection:**
   - **Description:** Continuously monitor critical infrastructure systems for security threats and anomalies. Implement detection capabilities to identify and respond to potential incidents promptly.
   - **Practices:** Use security information and event management (SIEM) solutions, deploy intrusion detection systems (IDS), conduct regular vulnerability scans, and establish real-time alerting.

5. **Patch Management and Updates:**
   - **Description:** Regularly update and patch software, firmware, and systems to address known vulnerabilities and improve security.
   - **Practices:** Implement a patch management program, prioritize patches based on risk, test patches in a controlled environment, and deploy updates in a timely manner.

6. **Incident Response and Recovery:**
   - **Description:** Develop and maintain an incident response plan to effectively manage

and mitigate cybersecurity incidents. Ensure that the plan includes procedures for recovery and restoration of critical infrastructure systems.

- ◦ **Practices:** Establish an incident response team (IRT), define roles and responsibilities, conduct regular incident response drills, and maintain backup and recovery solutions.

Strategies for Enhancing Resilience

Building resilience into critical infrastructure systems involves implementing strategies that ensure the continuity of operations and minimize the impact of cyber incidents. Key strategies for enhancing resilience include:

1. **Redundancy and Diversity:**
   - ◦ **Description:** Implement redundant systems and diverse pathways to ensure the continued availability of critical services in the event of a cyber incident.
   - ◦ **Practices:** Use backup power supplies, maintain alternative communication channels, deploy failover systems, and ensure diverse supply chain partners.

2. **Disaster Recovery Planning:**
   - ◦ **Description:** Develop and maintain disaster recovery plans that outline procedures for restoring critical infrastructure systems and services after a cyber incident or disaster.
   - ◦ **Practices:** Identify critical functions and dependencies, establish recovery time objectives (RTOs) and recovery point objectives (RPOs), conduct regular recovery drills, and ensure data backups are available and secure.

3. **Cybersecurity Awareness and Training:**

- **Description:** Educate and train employees and stakeholders about cybersecurity threats, best practices, and their roles in protecting critical infrastructure.
- **Practices:** Conduct regular security awareness training, provide role-specific training for OT and IT personnel, simulate phishing exercises, and promote a culture of security awareness.

4. **Collaboration and Information Sharing:**

- **Description:** Collaborate with industry partners, government agencies, and information-sharing organizations to exchange threat intelligence and best practices.
- **Practices:** Participate in Information Sharing and Analysis Centers (ISACs), engage with public-private partnerships, and establish communication protocols for sharing information during incidents.

5. **Regulatory Compliance and Standards:**

- **Description:** Ensure compliance with relevant regulations and standards to protect critical infrastructure and meet legal requirements.
- **Practices:** Stay informed about regulatory changes, implement security controls based on industry standards (e.g., NIST, IEC 62443), conduct regular audits, and maintain documentation for compliance reporting.

Conclusion

Securing critical infrastructure is vital to national security, public safety, and economic stability. By understanding the unique cybersecurity challenges faced by critical infrastructure and implementing best practices and strategies for risk assessment, access control, continuous monitoring, incident response, and resilience, operators can enhance the protection and resilience of these essential systems. This chapter provides valuable insights and practical guidance for securing critical infrastructure, offering a comprehensive approach to addressing the evolving cybersecurity landscape. As cyber threats continue to target critical infrastructure, the importance of proactive security measures and a collaborative approach in safeguarding these systems cannot be overstated.

CHAPTER 24: CYBERSECURITY FOR HEALTHCARE

Introduction

The healthcare industry is a prime target for cyberattacks due to the sensitive nature of the data it handles, including patient records, medical histories, and financial information. Ensuring the security of healthcare systems is critical to protect patient privacy, maintain trust, and comply with regulatory requirements. This chapter explores the unique cybersecurity challenges faced by the healthcare industry, best practices for securing healthcare environments, and strategies for safeguarding sensitive patient data.

Unique Cybersecurity Challenges in Healthcare

The healthcare industry faces several unique cybersecurity challenges that make it vulnerable to cyberattacks. Key challenges include:

1. **Sensitive Data:**
    - **Description:** Healthcare organizations handle highly sensitive data, including patient health records, medical histories, and financial information. The exposure of such data can lead to identity theft, fraud, and loss of patient trust.
    - **Impact:** Data breaches, financial loss,

reputational damage, and legal penalties.

2. **Legacy Systems and Devices:**
   - **Description:** Many healthcare facilities rely on outdated systems and medical devices that are no longer supported or updated. These legacy systems often have vulnerabilities that can be exploited by attackers.
   - **Impact:** Increased risk of cyberattacks, difficulty in implementing modern security measures, and potential for significant disruptions.

3. **Interoperability:**
   - **Description:** Healthcare systems often need to communicate and share data with various external entities, including insurance providers, pharmacies, and other healthcare facilities. Ensuring secure interoperability is a significant challenge.
   - **Impact:** Increased attack surface, potential for data breaches, and challenges in securing data exchanges.

4. **High-Pressure Environment:**
   - **Description:** Healthcare providers operate in high-pressure environments where quick access to information is critical for patient care. Cybersecurity measures must not hinder the efficiency and effectiveness of healthcare delivery.
   - **Impact:** Balancing security with usability, potential for delayed care, and risk of non-compliance with security protocols.

5. **Regulatory Compliance:**
   - **Description:** Healthcare organizations must

comply with strict regulatory requirements and standards designed to protect patient data and ensure data privacy.

- **Impact:** Resource-intensive compliance efforts, need for continuous monitoring and reporting, and challenges in keeping up with evolving regulations.

Best Practices for Securing Healthcare Environments

To address these challenges and enhance the cybersecurity of healthcare environments, organizations should implement a comprehensive set of best practices. Key best practices include:

1. **Implement Strong Access Controls:**
   - **Description:** Enforce strict access controls to ensure that only authorized personnel can access patient data and critical systems.
   - **Practices:** Use role-based access control (RBAC), implement multi-factor authentication (MFA), enforce least privilege access, and regularly review access permissions.

2. **Encrypt Sensitive Data:**
   - **Description:** Encrypt sensitive data at rest and in transit to protect it from unauthorized access and tampering.
   - **Practices:** Use strong encryption algorithms (e.g., AES-256), implement secure communication protocols (e.g., TLS/SSL), and ensure encryption for both stored and transmitted data.

3. **Regularly Update and Patch Systems:**
   - **Description:** Ensure that all systems, software, and medical devices are regularly updated and patched to address known

vulnerabilities and improve security.

- ○ **Practices:** Implement a patch management program, prioritize patches based on risk, test patches in a controlled environment, and deploy updates promptly.

4. **Conduct Security Awareness Training:**

- ○ **Description:** Educate healthcare staff about cybersecurity threats and best practices to reduce the risk of human error and improve overall security awareness.

- ○ **Practices:** Conduct regular security training sessions, provide phishing simulation exercises, share security tips and guidelines, and encourage employees to report suspicious activities.

5. **Secure Medical Devices:**

- ○ **Description:** Protect medical devices from cyber threats by implementing security measures that address their unique vulnerabilities and requirements.

- ○ **Practices:** Conduct risk assessments for medical devices, use network segmentation to isolate devices, implement device-level encryption, and ensure secure configurations.

6. **Develop an Incident Response Plan:**

- ○ **Description:** Establish an incident response plan to effectively manage and mitigate cybersecurity incidents. A well-defined plan ensures a coordinated and timely response to cyber threats.

- ○ **Practices:** Define roles and responsibilities, establish communication protocols, conduct incident response drills, and document incident response procedures.

Strategies for Safeguarding Patient Data

Protecting sensitive patient data is a critical aspect of healthcare cybersecurity. Organizations must implement measures to ensure the confidentiality, integrity, and availability of patient data. Key strategies for safeguarding patient data include:

1. **Data Loss Prevention (DLP):**
   - **Description:** Implement data loss prevention (DLP) solutions to monitor and protect sensitive data from being accidentally or maliciously leaked.
   - **Practices:** Use DLP tools to monitor data transfers, enforce policies for handling sensitive data, and block unauthorized access to data.

2. **Backup and Recovery:**
   - **Description:** Regularly backup critical data to protect against data loss due to cyberattacks, hardware failures, or other disasters. Ensure that backups are stored securely and can be easily restored.
   - **Practices:** Implement automated backup solutions, store backups in multiple locations (e.g., cloud, offsite storage), test backup and restore processes regularly, and encrypt backup data.

3. **Secure Data Exchanges:**
   - **Description:** Ensure that data exchanges between healthcare systems and external entities are secure to protect sensitive information.
   - **Practices:** Use secure communication channels (e.g., secure email, VPNs), implement data-sharing agreements with

external partners, and monitor data exchanges for compliance with security policies.

4. **Audit and Monitor Access to Patient Data:**
   ◦ **Description:** Continuously audit and monitor access to patient data to detect and respond to unauthorized access and potential security breaches.
   ◦ **Practices:** Use logging and monitoring solutions to track access to patient data, conduct regular audits, and establish real-time alerting for suspicious activities.

Compliance and Regulatory Considerations

Healthcare organizations must ensure that they comply with relevant regulations and standards to protect patient data and maintain legal and regulatory compliance. Key considerations include:

1. **Health Insurance Portability and Accountability Act (HIPAA):**
   ◦ **Description:** HIPAA sets standards for protecting the privacy and security of health information in the United States. It applies to healthcare providers, insurers, and their business associates.
   ◦ **Requirements:** Implement administrative, physical, and technical safeguards, ensure data confidentiality and integrity, conduct regular risk assessments, and report security incidents.

2. **General Data Protection Regulation (GDPR):**
   ◦ **Description:** GDPR sets standards for data protection and privacy for individuals within the European Union (EU). Healthcare organizations that process personal data

of EU residents must comply with GDPR requirements.

- **Requirements:** Implement data protection measures, obtain consent for data processing, provide data access and deletion rights, and report data breaches within 72 hours.

3. **National Institute of Standards and Technology (NIST) Cybersecurity Framework:**

- **Description:** The NIST Cybersecurity Framework provides a set of guidelines and best practices for managing cybersecurity risks. It is widely used by healthcare organizations to enhance their security posture.
- **Components:** Identify, Protect, Detect, Respond, Recover.

Conclusion

Securing healthcare environments is essential to protect sensitive patient data, maintain trust, and comply with regulatory requirements. By understanding the unique cybersecurity challenges faced by the healthcare industry and implementing best practices and strategies for access control, data encryption, system updates, security awareness, and incident response, healthcare organizations can enhance their cybersecurity posture and safeguard patient information. This chapter provides valuable insights and practical guidance for securing healthcare environments, offering a comprehensive approach to addressing the evolving cybersecurity landscape. As cyber threats continue to target the healthcare industry, the importance of proactive security measures in protecting patient data and ensuring the continuity of care cannot be overstated.

CHAPTER 25: CYBERSECURITY FOR FINANCIAL SERVICES

Introduction

The financial services industry is a prime target for cyberattacks due to the high value of the data and assets it handles, including financial transactions, customer information, and proprietary data. Ensuring the security of financial institutions is critical to protect sensitive data, maintain trust, and comply with regulatory requirements. This chapter explores the unique cybersecurity challenges faced by the financial services industry, best practices for securing financial environments, and strategies for safeguarding sensitive financial data.

Unique Cybersecurity Challenges in Financial Services

The financial services industry faces several unique cybersecurity challenges that make it vulnerable to cyberattacks. Key challenges include:

1. **High-Value Targets:**
   - **Description:** Financial institutions handle high-value data and assets, making them attractive targets for cybercriminals seeking financial gain, sensitive information, or disruption of services.
   - **Impact:** Financial losses, data breaches, reputational damage, and regulatory

penalties.

2. **Complex IT Environments:**
    - **Description:** Financial institutions often have complex IT environments with interconnected systems, legacy infrastructure, and third-party service providers. Securing these environments can be challenging.
    - **Impact:** Increased attack surface, potential for vulnerabilities, and difficulty in implementing consistent security measures.

3. **Sophisticated Threat Actors:**
    - **Description:** Financial institutions are targeted by sophisticated threat actors, including nation-state adversaries, organized crime groups, and cybercriminals with advanced capabilities.
    - **Impact:** Increased likelihood of targeted attacks, potential for prolonged and stealthy intrusions, and higher risk of significant financial impact.

4. **Regulatory Compliance:**
    - **Description:** Financial institutions must comply with a wide range of regulatory requirements and standards designed to protect customer data and ensure the security and integrity of financial systems.
    - **Impact:** Resource-intensive compliance efforts, need for continuous monitoring and reporting, and challenges in keeping up with evolving regulations.

5. **Real-Time Transactions:**
    - **Description:** The financial services industry

relies on real-time transactions and services, requiring robust security measures that do not hinder the speed and efficiency of operations.

- ◦ **Impact:** Balancing security with usability, potential for delayed transactions, and risk of non-compliance with security protocols.

Best Practices for Securing Financial Environments

To address these challenges and enhance the cybersecurity of financial environments, organizations should implement a comprehensive set of best practices. Key best practices include:

1. **Implement Strong Access Controls:**
   - ◦ **Description:** Enforce strict access controls to ensure that only authorized personnel can access financial systems and sensitive data.
   - ◦ **Practices:** Use role-based access control (RBAC), implement multi-factor authentication (MFA), enforce least privilege access, and regularly review access permissions.

2. **Encrypt Financial Data:**
   - ◦ **Description:** Encrypt financial data at rest and in transit to protect it from unauthorized access and tampering.
   - ◦ **Practices:** Use strong encryption algorithms (e.g., AES-256), implement secure communication protocols (e.g., TLS/SSL), and ensure encryption for both stored and transmitted data.

3. **Monitor and Detect Threats:**
   - ◦ **Description:** Continuously monitor financial systems for security threats and anomalies. Implement detection capabilities to identify

and respond to potential incidents promptly.

- **Practices:** Use security information and event management (SIEM) solutions, deploy intrusion detection systems (IDS), conduct regular vulnerability scans, and establish real-time alerting.

4. **Regularly Update and Patch Systems:**

- **Description:** Ensure that all systems, software, and applications are regularly updated and patched to address known vulnerabilities and improve security.

- **Practices:** Implement a patch management program, prioritize patches based on risk, test patches in a controlled environment, and deploy updates promptly.

5. **Conduct Security Awareness Training:**

- **Description:** Educate financial institution staff about cybersecurity threats and best practices to reduce the risk of human error and improve overall security awareness.

- **Practices:** Conduct regular security training sessions, provide phishing simulation exercises, share security tips and guidelines, and encourage employees to report suspicious activities.

6. **Develop an Incident Response Plan:**

- **Description:** Establish an incident response plan to effectively manage and mitigate cybersecurity incidents. A well-defined plan ensures a coordinated and timely response to cyber threats.

- **Practices:** Define roles and responsibilities, establish communication protocols, conduct incident response drills, and document incident response procedures.

Strategies for Safeguarding Financial Data

Protecting sensitive financial data is a critical aspect of financial services cybersecurity. Organizations must implement measures to ensure the confidentiality, integrity, and availability of financial data. Key strategies for safeguarding financial data include:

1. **Data Loss Prevention (DLP):**

   - **Description:** Implement data loss prevention (DLP) solutions to monitor and protect sensitive financial data from being accidentally or maliciously leaked.

   - **Practices:** Use DLP tools to monitor data transfers, enforce policies for handling sensitive data, and block unauthorized access to data.

2. **Secure Payment Processing:**

   - **Description:** Ensure that payment processing systems are secure to protect against fraud and unauthorized transactions.

   - **Practices:** Use secure payment gateways, implement tokenization and encryption for payment data, conduct regular security audits, and monitor for suspicious transaction patterns.

3. **Backup and Recovery:**

   - **Description:** Regularly backup critical financial data to protect against data loss due to cyberattacks, hardware failures, or other disasters. Ensure that backups are stored securely and can be easily restored.

   - **Practices:** Implement automated backup solutions, store backups in multiple locations (e.g., cloud, offsite storage), test backup and restore processes regularly, and encrypt backup data.

4. **Third-Party Risk Management:**
    - **Description:** Assess the security practices of third-party vendors and service providers to ensure they meet the organization's cybersecurity standards.
    - **Practices:** Conduct due diligence, require security assessments and certifications, include security requirements in contracts, and monitor third-party activities for compliance.

Compliance and Regulatory Considerations

Financial institutions must ensure that they comply with relevant regulations and standards to protect financial data and maintain legal and regulatory compliance. Key considerations include:

1. **Gramm-Leach-Bliley Act (GLBA):**
    - **Description:** GLBA requires financial institutions to protect the privacy and security of customer information. It mandates the implementation of administrative, technical, and physical safeguards.
    - **Requirements:** Develop a comprehensive information security program, conduct risk assessments, implement security controls, and ensure compliance with GLBA's Safeguards Rule.

2. **Payment Card Industry Data Security Standard (PCI DSS):**
    - **Description:** PCI DSS sets security standards for organizations that handle credit card

transactions. It aims to protect cardholder data and prevent data breaches.

- **Requirements:** Implement strong access controls, encrypt cardholder data, maintain secure systems and applications, and conduct regular security testing and monitoring.

3. **General Data Protection Regulation (GDPR):**

- **Description:** GDPR sets standards for data protection and privacy for individuals within the European Union (EU). Financial institutions that process personal data of EU residents must comply with GDPR requirements.

- **Requirements:** Implement data protection measures, obtain consent for data processing, provide data access and deletion rights, and report data breaches within 72 hours.

4. **National Institute of Standards and Technology (NIST) Cybersecurity Framework:**

- **Description:** The NIST Cybersecurity Framework provides a set of guidelines and best practices for managing cybersecurity risks. It is widely used by financial institutions to enhance their security posture.

- **Components:** Identify, Protect, Detect, Respond, Recover.

Conclusion

Securing financial environments is essential to protect sensitive financial data, maintain trust, and comply with regulatory requirements. By understanding the unique cybersecurity challenges faced by the financial services industry and implementing best practices and strategies for access control, data encryption, threat monitoring, system updates, security awareness, and incident response, financial institutions can enhance their cybersecurity posture and safeguard financial information. This chapter provides valuable insights and practical guidance for securing financial environments, offering a comprehensive approach to addressing the evolving cybersecurity landscape. As cyber threats continue to target the financial services industry, the importance of proactive security measures in protecting financial data and ensuring the continuity of financial operations cannot be overstated.

CHAPTER 26: CYBERSECURITY FOR EDUCATION

Introduction

The education sector is increasingly reliant on digital technologies for teaching, learning, and administration. While these technologies offer numerous benefits, they also introduce new cybersecurity challenges. Ensuring the security of educational institutions is essential to protect sensitive data, maintain trust, and support a safe learning environment. This chapter explores the unique cybersecurity challenges faced by the education sector, best practices for securing educational environments, and strategies for safeguarding student and staff data.

Unique Cybersecurity Challenges in Education

Educational institutions face several unique cybersecurity challenges that make them vulnerable to cyberattacks. Key challenges include:

1. **Diverse User Base:**
    - **Description:** Educational institutions have a diverse user base, including students, faculty, staff, and administrators, each with varying levels of cybersecurity awareness.
    - **Impact:** Increased risk of human error, potential for weak security practices, and

difficulty in enforcing consistent security measures.

2. **Sensitive Data:**

   ◦ **Description:** Educational institutions handle a wide range of sensitive data, including student records, financial information, and research data. The exposure of such data can lead to identity theft, fraud, and loss of trust.

   ◦ **Impact:** Data breaches, financial loss, reputational damage, and legal penalties.

3. **Open Networks:**

   ◦ **Description:** Many educational institutions offer open or semi-open networks to support learning and collaboration. These networks can be easily accessed by unauthorized users if not properly secured.

   ◦ **Impact:** Increased attack surface, potential for unauthorized access, and difficulty in securing network endpoints.

4. **Legacy Systems and Applications:**

   ◦ **Description:** Educational institutions often rely on legacy systems and applications that may have inherent vulnerabilities and lack modern security features.

   ◦ **Impact:** Increased risk of cyberattacks, difficulty in implementing security measures, and potential for significant disruptions.

5. **Remote Learning and BYOD:**

   ◦ **Description:** The rise of remote learning and bring-your-own-device (BYOD) policies introduces new security challenges as students and staff access institutional resources from various devices and locations.

- **Impact:** Increased complexity in managing security, potential for insecure devices, and challenges in monitoring and controlling access.

Best Practices for Securing Educational Environments

To address these challenges and enhance the cybersecurity of educational environments, institutions should implement a comprehensive set of best practices. Key best practices include:

1. **Implement Strong Access Controls:**
   - **Description:** Enforce strict access controls to ensure that only authorized users can access sensitive data and institutional resources.
   - **Practices:** Use role-based access control (RBAC), implement multi-factor authentication (MFA), enforce least privilege access, and regularly review access permissions.

2. **Encrypt Sensitive Data:**
   - **Description:** Encrypt sensitive data at rest and in transit to protect it from unauthorized access and tampering.
   - **Practices:** Use strong encryption algorithms (e.g., AES-256), implement secure communication protocols (e.g., TLS/SSL), and ensure encryption for both stored and transmitted data.

3. **Secure Networks:**
   - **Description:** Protect institutional networks from unauthorized access and cyber threats by implementing robust security measures.
   - **Practices:** Use firewalls to control incoming and outgoing traffic, implement network segmentation to isolate sensitive systems,

configure wireless networks securely, and use virtual private networks (VPNs) for remote access.

4. **Conduct Security Awareness Training:**
   ○ **Description:** Educate students, faculty, and staff about cybersecurity threats and best practices to reduce the risk of human error and improve overall security awareness.
   ○ **Practices:** Conduct regular security training sessions, provide phishing simulation exercises, share security tips and guidelines, and encourage reporting of suspicious activities.

5. **Regularly Update and Patch Systems:**
   ○ **Description:** Ensure that all systems, software, and applications are regularly updated and patched to address known vulnerabilities and improve security.
   ○ **Practices:** Implement a patch management program, prioritize patches based on risk, test patches in a controlled environment, and deploy updates promptly.

6. **Develop an Incident Response Plan:**
   ○ **Description:** Establish an incident response plan to effectively manage and mitigate cybersecurity incidents. A well-defined plan ensures a coordinated and timely response to cyber threats.
   ○ **Practices:** Define roles and responsibilities, establish communication protocols, conduct incident response drills, and document incident response procedures.

Strategies for Safeguarding Student and Staff Data

Protecting sensitive student and staff data is a critical aspect of education cybersecurity. Institutions must implement measures to ensure the confidentiality, integrity, and availability of this data. Key strategies for safeguarding student and staff data include:

1. **Data Loss Prevention (DLP):**
   - **Description:** Implement data loss prevention (DLP) solutions to monitor and protect sensitive data from being accidentally or maliciously leaked.
   - **Practices:** Use DLP tools to monitor data transfers, enforce policies for handling sensitive data, and block unauthorized access to data.

2. **Backup and Recovery:**
   - **Description:** Regularly backup critical data to protect against data loss due to cyberattacks, hardware failures, or other disasters. Ensure that backups are stored securely and can be easily restored.
   - **Practices:** Implement automated backup solutions, store backups in multiple locations (e.g., cloud, offsite storage), test backup and restore processes regularly, and encrypt backup data.

3. **Secure Data Exchanges:**
   - **Description:** Ensure that data exchanges between educational systems and external entities are secure to protect sensitive information.
   - **Practices:** Use secure communication channels (e.g., secure email, VPNs), implement data-sharing agreements with external partners, and monitor data

exchanges for compliance with security policies.

4. **Audit and Monitor Access to Data:**
   - **Description:** Continuously audit and monitor access to student and staff data to detect and respond to unauthorized access and potential security breaches.
   - **Practices:** Use logging and monitoring solutions to track access to sensitive data, conduct regular audits, and establish real-time alerting for suspicious activities.

Compliance and Regulatory Considerations

Educational institutions must ensure that they comply with relevant regulations and standards to protect sensitive data and maintain legal and regulatory compliance. Key considerations include:

1. **Family Educational Rights and Privacy Act (FERPA):**
   - **Description:** FERPA sets standards for the privacy and protection of student education records in the United States. Educational institutions must comply with FERPA requirements when handling student records.
   - **Requirements:** Protect the confidentiality of student records, obtain consent for data sharing, provide access to records for students and parents, and ensure compliance with FERPA's privacy provisions.

2. **General Data Protection Regulation (GDPR):**
   - **Description:** GDPR sets standards for data protection and privacy for individuals within the European Union (EU). Educational institutions that process personal data of EU residents must comply with GDPR requirements.

- ○ **Requirements:** Implement data protection measures, obtain consent for data processing, provide data access and deletion rights, and report data breaches within 72 hours.

3. **Children's Online Privacy Protection Act (COPPA):**

- ○ **Description:** COPPA sets standards for the online privacy and protection of children under the age of 13 in the United States. Educational institutions must comply with COPPA requirements when collecting personal information from children.
- ○ **Requirements:** Obtain parental consent for data collection, provide notice of data practices, ensure data security, and comply with COPPA's privacy provisions.

Conclusion

Securing educational environments is essential to protect sensitive student and staff data, maintain trust, and support a safe learning environment. By understanding the unique cybersecurity challenges faced by the education sector and implementing best practices and strategies for access control, data encryption, network security, security awareness, and incident response, educational institutions can enhance their cybersecurity posture and safeguard sensitive information. This chapter provides valuable insights and practical guidance for securing educational environments, offering a comprehensive approach to addressing the evolving cybersecurity landscape. As cyber threats continue to target the education sector, the importance of proactive security measures in protecting student and staff data and ensuring the continuity of education cannot be overstated.

CHAPTER 27: CYBERSECURITY FOR GOVERNMENT AND PUBLIC SECTOR

Introduction

Government and public sector organizations are prime targets for cyberattacks due to the sensitive information they handle and their critical role in maintaining national security and public safety. Ensuring the cybersecurity of government systems is crucial to protect sensitive data, maintain public trust, and ensure the continuity of essential services. This chapter explores the unique cybersecurity challenges faced by government and public sector organizations, best practices for securing these environments, and strategies for safeguarding sensitive information.

Unique Cybersecurity Challenges in Government and Public Sector

Government and public sector organizations face several unique cybersecurity challenges that make them vulnerable to cyberattacks. Key challenges include:

1. **Sensitive Data:**
    ◦ **Description:** Government agencies handle highly sensitive information, including personal data of citizens, classified

information, and critical infrastructure data. The exposure of such data can lead to national security threats, identity theft, and loss of public trust.

- **Impact:** Data breaches, financial loss, reputational damage, and legal penalties.

2. **Complex IT Environments:**

- **Description:** Government organizations often have complex IT environments with interconnected systems, legacy infrastructure, and multiple stakeholders. Securing these environments can be challenging.
- **Impact:** Increased attack surface, potential for vulnerabilities, and difficulty in implementing consistent security measures.

3. **Sophisticated Threat Actors:**

- **Description:** Government and public sector organizations are targeted by sophisticated threat actors, including nation-state adversaries, hacktivists, and cybercriminals with advanced capabilities.
- **Impact:** Increased likelihood of targeted attacks, potential for prolonged and stealthy intrusions, and higher risk of significant impact on national security.

4. **Regulatory Compliance:**

- **Description:** Government organizations must comply with a wide range of regulatory requirements and standards designed to protect sensitive data and ensure the security and integrity of government systems.
- **Impact:** Resource-intensive compliance efforts, need for continuous monitoring and

reporting, and challenges in keeping up with evolving regulations.

5. **Critical Infrastructure Protection:**

   ◦ **Description:** Government agencies are responsible for protecting critical infrastructure sectors, such as energy, water, transportation, and healthcare, from cyber threats.

   ◦ **Impact:** Potential for widespread disruptions, economic impact, and threats to public safety.

Best Practices for Securing Government and Public Sector Environments

To address these challenges and enhance the cybersecurity of government and public sector environments, organizations should implement a comprehensive set of best practices. Key best practices include:

1. **Implement Strong Access Controls:**

   ◦ **Description:** Enforce strict access controls to ensure that only authorized personnel can access sensitive data and government systems.

   ◦ **Practices:** Use role-based access control (RBAC), implement multi-factor authentication (MFA), enforce least privilege access, and regularly review access permissions.

2. **Encrypt Sensitive Data:**

   ◦ **Description:** Encrypt sensitive data at rest and in transit to protect it from unauthorized access and tampering.

   ◦ **Practices:** Use strong encryption algorithms (e.g., AES-256), implement secure communication protocols (e.g., TLS/SSL), and ensure encryption for both stored and transmitted data.

3. **Monitor and Detect Threats:**
   ◦ **Description:** Continuously monitor government systems for security threats and anomalies. Implement detection capabilities to identify and respond to potential incidents promptly.
   ◦ **Practices:** Use security information and event management (SIEM) solutions, deploy intrusion detection systems (IDS), conduct regular vulnerability scans, and establish real-time alerting.

4. **Regularly Update and Patch Systems:**
   ◦ **Description:** Ensure that all systems, software, and applications are regularly updated and patched to address known vulnerabilities and improve security.
   ◦ **Practices:** Implement a patch management program, prioritize patches based on risk, test patches in a controlled environment, and deploy updates promptly.

5. **Conduct Security Awareness Training:**
   ◦ **Description:** Educate government employees and stakeholders about cybersecurity threats and best practices to reduce the risk of human error and improve overall security awareness.
   ◦ **Practices:** Conduct regular security training sessions, provide phishing simulation exercises, share security tips and guidelines, and encourage employees to report suspicious activities.

6. **Develop an Incident Response Plan:**

- **Description:** Establish an incident response plan to effectively manage and mitigate cybersecurity incidents. A well-defined plan ensures a coordinated and timely response to cyber threats.
- **Practices:** Define roles and responsibilities, establish communication protocols, conduct incident response drills, and document incident response procedures.

Strategies for Safeguarding Sensitive Information

Protecting sensitive government information is a critical aspect of public sector cybersecurity. Organizations must implement measures to ensure the confidentiality, integrity, and availability of sensitive data. Key strategies for safeguarding sensitive information include:

1. **Data Loss Prevention (DLP):**
   - **Description:** Implement data loss prevention (DLP) solutions to monitor and protect sensitive data from being accidentally or maliciously leaked.
   - **Practices:** Use DLP tools to monitor data transfers, enforce policies for handling sensitive data, and block unauthorized access to data.

2. **Backup and Recovery:**
   - **Description:** Regularly backup critical data to protect against data loss due to cyberattacks, hardware failures, or other disasters. Ensure that backups are stored securely and can be easily restored.
   - **Practices:** Implement automated backup solutions, store backups in multiple locations (e.g., cloud, offsite storage), test backup and restore processes regularly, and encrypt

backup data.

3. **Secure Data Exchanges:**
   - **Description:** Ensure that data exchanges between government systems and external entities are secure to protect sensitive information.
   - **Practices:** Use secure communication channels (e.g., secure email, VPNs), implement data-sharing agreements with external partners, and monitor data exchanges for compliance with security policies.

4. **Audit and Monitor Access to Data:**
   - **Description:** Continuously audit and monitor access to sensitive government data to detect and respond to unauthorized access and potential security breaches.
   - **Practices:** Use logging and monitoring solutions to track access to sensitive data, conduct regular audits, and establish real-time alerting for suspicious activities.

Compliance and Regulatory Considerations

Government and public sector organizations must ensure that they comply with relevant regulations and standards to protect sensitive data and maintain legal and regulatory compliance. Key considerations include:

1. **Federal Information Security Management Act (FISMA):**
   - **Description:** FISMA sets standards for protecting the information and information systems of federal government agencies in the United States. It mandates the implementation of security controls and continuous monitoring.

- **Requirements:** Develop and implement an information security program, conduct risk assessments, implement security controls based on NIST standards, and conduct continuous monitoring and reporting.

2. **General Data Protection Regulation (GDPR):**
   - **Description:** GDPR sets standards for data protection and privacy for individuals within the European Union (EU). Government organizations that process personal data of EU residents must comply with GDPR requirements.
   - **Requirements:** Implement data protection measures, obtain consent for data processing, provide data access and deletion rights, and report data breaches within 72 hours.

3. **National Institute of Standards and Technology (NIST) Cybersecurity Framework:**
   - **Description:** The NIST Cybersecurity Framework provides a set of guidelines and best practices for managing cybersecurity risks. It is widely used by government organizations to enhance their security posture.
   - **Components:** Identify, Protect, Detect, Respond, Recover.

4. **International Organization for Standardization (ISO) Standards:**
   - **Description:** ISO standards, such as ISO/IEC 27001, provide guidelines for information security management systems (ISMS) and are used by government organizations to achieve and maintain high security standards.
   - **Requirements:** Implement an ISMS, conduct

risk assessments, establish security controls, conduct internal audits, and achieve ISO certification.

Conclusion

Securing government and public sector environments is essential to protect sensitive information, maintain public trust, and ensure the continuity of essential services. By understanding the unique cybersecurity challenges faced by government organizations and implementing best practices and strategies for access control, data encryption, threat monitoring, system updates, security awareness, and incident response, government entities can enhance their cybersecurity posture and safeguard sensitive information. This chapter provides valuable insights and practical guidance for securing government and public sector environments, offering a comprehensive approach to addressing the evolving cybersecurity landscape. As cyber threats continue to target government and public sector organizations, the importance of proactive security measures in protecting sensitive data and ensuring the continuity of government operations cannot be overstated.

CHAPTER 28: THE ROLE OF ARTIFICIAL INTELLIGENCE IN CYBERSECURITY

Introduction

Artificial Intelligence (AI) is rapidly transforming the field of cybersecurity by providing advanced tools and techniques for threat detection, analysis, and response. AI has the potential to enhance the effectiveness of cybersecurity measures, reduce the workload of security professionals, and improve the overall security posture of organizations. This chapter explores the role of AI in cybersecurity, key applications and benefits, challenges and limitations, and future trends in AI-driven security solutions.

Key Applications of AI in Cybersecurity

AI technologies are being applied in various aspects of cybersecurity to enhance threat detection, response, and prevention. Key applications of AI in cybersecurity include:

1. **Threat Detection and Analysis:**
   - **Description:** AI algorithms can analyze vast amounts of data to identify patterns and anomalies indicative of cyber threats. Machine learning models can be trained to detect previously unknown threats by

recognizing unusual behaviors.

- **Applications:** Intrusion detection systems (IDS), security information and event management (SIEM) solutions, endpoint detection and response (EDR) tools, network traffic analysis.

2. **Behavioral Analytics:**

- **Description:** AI can analyze user behavior to establish baselines of normal activity and identify deviations that may indicate malicious activity. Behavioral analytics helps detect insider threats and compromised accounts.

- **Applications:** User and entity behavior analytics (UEBA), fraud detection systems, anomaly detection in authentication and access patterns.

3. **Automated Incident Response:**

- **Description:** AI-powered systems can automate incident response processes, enabling rapid and efficient handling of security incidents. Automated response can include actions such as isolating affected systems, blocking malicious traffic, and notifying relevant personnel.

- **Applications:** Security orchestration, automation, and response (SOAR) platforms, automated malware analysis, real-time threat mitigation.

4. **Vulnerability Management:**

- **Description:** AI can assist in identifying and prioritizing vulnerabilities based on risk, helping organizations focus their remediation efforts on the most critical issues.

○ **Applications:** Vulnerability scanning and assessment tools, predictive vulnerability analytics, automated patch management.

5. **Phishing Detection and Prevention:**

○ **Description:** AI can analyze email content and sender behavior to detect phishing attempts and prevent them from reaching end-users.

○ **Applications:** Email security gateways, anti-phishing tools, real-time phishing detection systems.

Benefits of AI in Cybersecurity

The integration of AI into cybersecurity offers several significant benefits:

1. **Enhanced Threat Detection:**

○ **Description:** AI's ability to analyze large datasets and identify patterns allows for more accurate and timely detection of cyber threats. Machine learning models can continuously improve their detection capabilities based on new data.

○ **Benefits:** Reduced false positives, improved detection of previously unknown threats, faster identification of security incidents.

2. **Increased Efficiency:**

○ **Description:** AI-powered automation can streamline security operations and reduce the manual workload of security teams. Automated processes enable faster response times and allow security professionals to focus on higher-priority tasks.

○ **Benefits:** Enhanced productivity, quicker incident response, reduced operational costs.

3. **Proactive Threat Mitigation:**

- **Description:** AI's predictive capabilities enable organizations to anticipate and mitigate threats before they escalate into major incidents. Machine learning models can identify potential attack vectors and vulnerabilities.
- **Benefits:** Improved proactive defense, reduced risk of successful attacks, better resource allocation.

4. **Scalability:**
   - **Description:** AI solutions can scale to handle the increasing volume and complexity of cyber threats. AI-driven security tools can analyze vast amounts of data in real-time, providing comprehensive coverage across large and distributed networks.
   - **Benefits:** Greater ability to manage and secure large-scale environments, improved adaptability to evolving threat landscapes.

5. **Continuous Improvement:**
   - **Description:** Machine learning models can continuously learn and adapt based on new data and evolving threat patterns. This enables ongoing improvement in the accuracy and effectiveness of AI-driven security solutions.
   - **Benefits:** Long-term enhancement of security capabilities, better alignment with emerging threats, reduced need for manual updates.

Challenges and Limitations of AI in Cybersecurity

While AI offers numerous benefits, it also presents challenges and limitations that must be addressed:

1. **Data Quality and Availability:**

- **Description:** AI models rely on high-quality data for training and analysis. Incomplete or biased data can lead to inaccurate results and reduced effectiveness.
- **Challenges:** Ensuring access to diverse and comprehensive datasets, addressing data quality issues, mitigating biases in data.

2. **Adversarial Attacks:**

- **Description:** Attackers can manipulate AI models by introducing malicious inputs designed to deceive the system and evade detection. Adversarial attacks pose a significant threat to AI-driven security solutions.
- **Challenges:** Developing robust defenses against adversarial attacks, implementing techniques for adversarial training, ensuring model resilience.

3. **Complexity and Interpretability:**

- **Description:** AI models, particularly deep learning models, can be complex and difficult to interpret. Lack of transparency in AI decision-making can hinder trust and accountability.
- **Challenges:** Improving model interpretability, providing explanations for AI decisions, ensuring transparency in AI-driven security processes.

4. **Resource Requirements:**

- **Description:** Training and deploying AI models can require significant computational resources and expertise. Smaller organizations may struggle to implement and maintain AI-driven security solutions.

- ○ **Challenges:** Addressing resource constraints, providing access to scalable and cost-effective AI solutions, offering training and support for AI implementation.

5. **Ethical and Privacy Considerations:**
   - ○ **Description:** The use of AI in cybersecurity raises ethical and privacy concerns, particularly regarding the collection and analysis of sensitive data. Ensuring ethical AI practices is essential for maintaining trust and compliance.
   - ○ **Challenges:** Implementing privacy-preserving AI techniques, ensuring ethical AI usage, adhering to regulatory requirements.

Future Trends in AI-Driven Cybersecurity

The future of AI in cybersecurity is shaped by ongoing advancements in technology and evolving threat landscapes. Key trends to watch for include:

1. **AI-Powered Threat Intelligence:**
   - ○ **Description:** The integration of AI with threat intelligence platforms will enable more accurate and timely analysis of threat data, providing organizations with actionable insights for proactive defense.
   - ○ **Future Impact:** Enhanced threat intelligence capabilities, improved anticipation of emerging threats, better-informed security strategies.

2. **Collaboration Between AI and Human Experts:**
   - ○ **Description:** AI-driven security solutions will increasingly complement human expertise, with AI handling routine tasks and humans focusing on complex decision-making and

strategic planning.

- **Future Impact:** Improved synergy between AI and human analysts, enhanced overall security effectiveness, reduced workload for security teams.

3. **Federated Learning and Privacy-Preserving AI:**

   - **Description:** Federated learning enables the training of AI models on decentralized data sources without sharing sensitive data. Privacy-preserving AI techniques will ensure that data privacy is maintained while leveraging AI capabilities.

   - **Future Impact:** Increased adoption of privacy-preserving AI, improved data security, broader access to AI-driven security solutions.

4. **AI for IoT Security:**

   - **Description:** As the Internet of Things (IoT) continues to grow, AI-driven security solutions will play a crucial role in protecting IoT devices and networks from cyber threats.

   - **Future Impact:** Enhanced IoT security, improved threat detection and response for connected devices, greater resilience against IoT-specific threats.

5. **Quantum-Resistant AI:**

   - **Description:** The development of AI-driven security solutions that are resistant to quantum computing threats will be essential as quantum technologies become more advanced.

   - **Future Impact:** Improved resilience against quantum-based attacks, enhanced long-term security, better preparation for future technological advancements.

Conclusion

Artificial Intelligence is revolutionizing the field of cybersecurity by providing advanced tools and techniques for threat detection, analysis, and response. While AI offers numerous benefits, it also presents challenges that must be addressed to ensure its effective and ethical use. By understanding the key applications, benefits, challenges, and future trends of AI in cybersecurity, organizations can leverage AI-driven solutions to enhance their security posture and stay ahead of evolving threats. This chapter provides a comprehensive overview of the role of AI in cybersecurity, offering valuable insights for cybersecurity professionals and organizations seeking to harness the power of AI in safeguarding digital assets. As AI continues to advance, its integration into cybersecurity will be essential for building a resilient and secure digital future.

CHAPTER 29: CYBERSECURITY FOR SMART CITIES

Introduction

The concept of smart cities is transforming urban living by integrating advanced technologies and data analytics to enhance the efficiency, sustainability, and quality of life in urban environments. Smart cities leverage the Internet of Things (IoT), artificial intelligence (AI), big data, and other cutting-edge technologies to optimize various aspects of city management, including transportation, energy, waste management, and public safety. However, the increased connectivity and data exchange in smart cities also introduce new cybersecurity challenges. This chapter explores the unique cybersecurity challenges faced by smart cities, best practices for securing smart city infrastructure, and strategies for safeguarding citizen data.

Unique Cybersecurity Challenges in Smart Cities

Smart cities face several unique cybersecurity challenges that must be addressed to ensure the security and resilience of urban infrastructure. Key challenges include:

1. **Vast Attack Surface:**
   - **Description:** The extensive network of interconnected devices, sensors, and systems in smart cities creates a vast attack surface that can be exploited by cybercriminals.

- **Impact:** Increased risk of cyberattacks, potential for widespread disruptions, and difficulty in monitoring and securing all endpoints.

2. **Data Privacy and Security:**
    - **Description:** Smart cities collect and process vast amounts of data, including personal information of citizens, which must be protected from unauthorized access and misuse.
    - **Impact:** Data breaches, privacy violations, loss of citizen trust, and legal penalties.

3. **Legacy Systems:**
    - **Description:** Many existing urban infrastructure systems were not designed with cybersecurity in mind and may lack modern security features.
    - **Impact:** Increased vulnerability to cyberattacks, challenges in integrating legacy systems with new technologies, and potential for security gaps.

4. **Interconnected Systems:**
    - **Description:** The interconnected nature of smart city systems means that a cyberattack on one component can have cascading effects on other systems.
    - **Impact:** Broader impact of cyberattacks, potential for multiple system failures, and challenges in isolating and containing incidents.

5. **Complex Governance and Coordination:**
    - **Description:** Smart city initiatives often involve multiple stakeholders, including

government agencies, private sector partners, and citizens, making governance and coordination complex.

- **Impact:** Difficulty in implementing consistent security measures, challenges in achieving stakeholder collaboration, and potential for gaps in accountability.

Best Practices for Securing Smart City Infrastructure

To address these challenges and enhance the cybersecurity of smart city infrastructure, city planners and stakeholders should implement a comprehensive set of best practices. Key best practices include:

1. **Implement Robust Access Controls:**
   - **Description:** Enforce strict access controls to ensure that only authorized personnel can access smart city systems and data.
   - **Practices:** Use role-based access control (RBAC), implement multi-factor authentication (MFA), enforce least privilege access, and regularly review access permissions.

2. **Encrypt Data at Rest and in Transit:**
   - **Description:** Encrypt data at rest and in transit to protect it from unauthorized access and tampering.
   - **Practices:** Use strong encryption algorithms (e.g., AES-256), implement secure communication protocols (e.g., TLS/SSL), and ensure encryption for both stored and transmitted data.

3. **Conduct Regular Security Assessments:**
   - **Description:** Perform regular security assessments to identify vulnerabilities and

assess the security posture of smart city systems.

- **Practices:** Conduct vulnerability scans, penetration testing, and security audits, prioritize remediation efforts based on risk, and continuously monitor for new threats.

4. **Secure IoT Devices and Networks:**
   - **Description:** Implement security measures to protect IoT devices and networks from cyber threats.
   - **Practices:** Use secure boot and firmware updates, implement device authentication and authorization, segment IoT networks from other critical networks, and monitor IoT traffic for anomalies.

5. **Develop an Incident Response Plan:**
   - **Description:** Establish an incident response plan to effectively manage and mitigate cybersecurity incidents in smart city infrastructure.
   - **Practices:** Define roles and responsibilities, establish communication protocols, conduct incident response drills, and document incident response procedures.

Strategies for Safeguarding Citizen Data

Protecting citizen data is a critical aspect of smart city cybersecurity. City planners and stakeholders must implement measures to ensure the confidentiality, integrity, and availability of citizen data. Key strategies for safeguarding citizen data include:

1. **Data Minimization:**
   - **Description:** Collect and process only the minimum amount of data necessary to

achieve smart city objectives.

- ◦ **Practices:** Implement data minimization principles, regularly review data collection practices, and ensure data retention policies are in place.

2. **Data Anonymization and De-identification:**

- ◦ **Description:** Anonymize and de-identify personal data to protect citizen privacy while still enabling data analysis and decision-making.

- ◦ **Practices:** Use data anonymization techniques, implement de-identification protocols, and ensure that re-identification risks are minimized.

3. **Data Governance and Privacy Policies:**

- ◦ **Description:** Establish data governance frameworks and privacy policies to ensure responsible data management and protection.

- ◦ **Practices:** Develop and communicate privacy policies, implement data access controls, conduct regular data privacy assessments, and ensure compliance with relevant regulations.

4. **Audit and Monitor Access to Data:**

- ◦ **Description:** Continuously audit and monitor access to citizen data to detect and respond to unauthorized access and potential security breaches.

- ◦ **Practices:** Use logging and monitoring solutions to track access to sensitive data, conduct regular audits, and establish real-time alerting for suspicious activities.

Building Resilience in Smart Cities

Building resilience into smart city infrastructure involves implementing strategies that ensure the continuity of services and minimize the impact of cyber incidents. Key strategies for building resilience include:

1. **Redundancy and Failover Systems:**
   - **Description:** Implement redundant systems and failover mechanisms to ensure the continued availability of critical services in the event of a cyber incident.
   - **Practices:** Use backup power supplies, maintain alternative communication channels, deploy failover systems, and ensure diverse supply chain partners.

2. **Disaster Recovery Planning:**
   - **Description:** Develop and maintain disaster recovery plans that outline procedures for restoring smart city services after a cyber incident or disaster.
   - **Practices:** Identify critical functions and dependencies, establish recovery time objectives (RTOs) and recovery point objectives (RPOs), conduct regular recovery drills, and ensure data backups are available and secure.

3. **Public-Private Partnerships:**
   - **Description:** Foster collaboration between public sector entities and private sector partners to enhance the security and resilience of smart city infrastructure.
   - **Practices:** Establish public-private partnerships, share threat intelligence and best practices, and coordinate efforts to address cybersecurity challenges.

4. **Community Engagement and Awareness:**
   - **Description:** Engage the community and raise awareness about smart city cybersecurity to promote responsible behaviors and foster a culture of security.
   - **Practices:** Conduct public awareness campaigns, provide cybersecurity education and resources, and encourage citizen participation in security initiatives.

Conclusion

Securing smart city infrastructure is essential to protect sensitive data, ensure the resilience of urban services, and maintain public trust. By understanding the unique cybersecurity challenges faced by smart cities and implementing best practices and strategies for access control, data encryption, security assessments, IoT protection, data governance, and resilience, city planners and stakeholders can enhance the cybersecurity posture of smart cities and safeguard citizen information. This chapter provides valuable insights and practical guidance for securing smart city environments, offering a comprehensive approach to addressing the evolving cybersecurity landscape. As smart cities continue to grow and evolve, the importance of proactive security measures in protecting urban infrastructure and ensuring the continuity of services cannot be overstated.

CHAPTER 30: PREPARING FOR THE FUTURE OF CYBERSECURITY

Introduction

As we look ahead, the future of cybersecurity is shaped by rapid technological advancements, evolving threat landscapes, and increasing regulatory demands. Preparing for the future of cybersecurity requires a forward-thinking approach, proactive strategies, and continuous adaptation to new challenges and opportunities. This chapter explores the key trends and considerations for the future of cybersecurity, offering insights and strategies to help organizations stay ahead and build a resilient security posture.

Emerging Cybersecurity Trends

Several key trends are expected to influence the future of cybersecurity. Understanding these trends can help organizations anticipate and prepare for new challenges. Key emerging trends include:

1. **Zero Trust Architecture:**
   - **Description:** The Zero Trust security model assumes that no entity, whether inside or outside the network, is inherently trustworthy. Every access request is

continuously verified, and the principle of least privilege is enforced.

- ○ **Impact:** Improved access control, reduced risk of lateral movement by attackers, and enhanced protection of critical assets.

2. **Artificial Intelligence and Machine Learning:**

- ○ **Description:** AI and ML technologies are becoming increasingly integral to cybersecurity, providing advanced tools for threat detection, analysis, and response. AI can analyze vast amounts of data and identify patterns that may indicate cyber threats.

- ○ **Impact:** Enhanced threat detection capabilities, reduced false positives, and faster incident response.

3. **Quantum Computing:**

- ○ **Description:** Quantum computing has the potential to break traditional encryption algorithms, posing a significant threat to data security. However, it also offers opportunities for developing quantum-resistant cryptography and enhancing security.

- ○ **Impact:** Need for quantum-resistant cryptographic algorithms, increased investment in quantum-safe security solutions, and potential for advanced threat detection capabilities.

4. **IoT Security:**

- ○ **Description:** The proliferation of Internet of Things (IoT) devices introduces new security challenges. Securing IoT environments is essential to protect sensitive data and ensure the reliability of connected systems.

○ **Impact:** Greater emphasis on device authentication, data encryption, and secure firmware updates, as well as the development of IoT-specific security frameworks.

5. **Cloud Security:**

   ○ **Description:** As organizations continue to migrate to the cloud, securing cloud environments becomes paramount. Cloud security involves protecting data, applications, and infrastructure hosted in cloud services.

   ○ **Impact:** Increased focus on cloud-native security solutions, greater emphasis on data encryption and access controls, and improved visibility into cloud activities.

Proactive Strategies for Future Cybersecurity

To stay ahead in the evolving cybersecurity landscape, organizations must adopt proactive strategies and continuously improve their security posture. Key proactive strategies include:

1. **Continuous Learning and Training:**

   ○ **Description:** Stay informed about the latest cybersecurity trends, threats, and best practices through continuous learning and training. Regularly update skills and knowledge to stay current.

   ○ **Practices:** Attend industry conferences, participate in training programs, obtain relevant certifications, and engage with cybersecurity communities.

2. **Implementing Advanced Security Technologies:**

   ○ **Description:** Leverage advanced security technologies, such as AI and ML, to enhance threat detection, analysis, and response capabilities.

- Practices: Invest in AI-powered security solutions, implement automated threat detection and response, and use predictive analytics to anticipate and mitigate threats.

3. **Adopting a Zero Trust Approach:**

- Description: Implement a Zero Trust security model to enhance access controls and minimize the attack surface. Continuously verify the identity of users and devices.

- Practices: Use multi-factor authentication (MFA), implement micro-segmentation, enforce least privilege access, and monitor all network activities.

4. **Enhancing Threat Intelligence:**

- Description: Utilize threat intelligence to stay informed about emerging threats and attack vectors. Integrate threat intelligence into security operations to improve threat detection and response.

- Practices: Subscribe to threat intelligence feeds, participate in information-sharing networks, and use threat intelligence platforms.

5. **Strengthening Incident Response Capabilities:**

- Description: Develop and maintain robust incident response capabilities to effectively manage and mitigate security incidents. Ensure that incident response plans are regularly tested and updated.

- Practices: Establish an incident response team (IRT), conduct regular incident response drills, use incident response automation, and perform post-incident reviews.

Building a Resilient Security Posture

Building a resilient security posture involves implementing strategies that ensure the continuity of operations and minimize the impact of cyber incidents. Key strategies for building resilience include:

1. **Redundancy and Diversity:**
   - **Description:** Implement redundant systems and diverse pathways to ensure the continued availability of critical services in the event of a cyber incident.
   - **Practices:** Use backup power supplies, maintain alternative communication channels, deploy failover systems, and ensure diverse supply chain partners.

2. **Disaster Recovery Planning:**
   - **Description:** Develop and maintain disaster recovery plans that outline procedures for restoring critical systems and services after a cyber incident or disaster.
   - **Practices:** Identify critical functions and dependencies, establish recovery time objectives (RTOs) and recovery point objectives (RPOs), conduct regular recovery drills, and ensure data backups are available and secure.

3. **Public-Private Partnerships:**
   - **Description:** Foster collaboration between public sector entities and private sector partners to enhance the security and resilience of critical infrastructure.
   - **Practices:** Establish public-private partnerships, share threat intelligence and best practices, and coordinate efforts to

address cybersecurity challenges.

4. **Community Engagement and Awareness:**

   ○ **Description:** Engage the community and raise awareness about cybersecurity to promote responsible behaviors and foster a culture of security.

   ○ **Practices:** Conduct public awareness campaigns, provide cybersecurity education and resources, and encourage citizen participation in security initiatives.

Future-Proofing Cybersecurity

Future-proofing cybersecurity involves anticipating and preparing for future threats and challenges. Key considerations for future-proofing cybersecurity include:

1. **Investing in Research and Development:**

   ○ **Description:** Invest in research and development to explore new security technologies, methodologies, and best practices.

   ○ **Practices:** Collaborate with academic institutions, support cybersecurity research initiatives, and stay informed about emerging technologies.

2. **Adopting Flexible and Adaptive Security Frameworks:**

   ○ **Description:** Implement flexible and adaptive security frameworks that can evolve with changing threats and technological advancements.

   ○ **Practices:** Use modular security architectures, adopt agile security practices, and regularly review and update security policies and procedures.

3. **Emphasizing Cyber Resilience:**
   - **Description:** Focus on building cyber resilience to ensure that organizations can withstand and recover from cyber incidents.
   - **Practices:** Implement resilience-focused security measures, conduct regular resilience assessments, and develop comprehensive recovery plans.

4. **Preparing for Regulatory Changes:**
   - **Description:** Stay informed about regulatory changes and ensure compliance with evolving cybersecurity and data protection regulations.
   - **Practices:** Monitor regulatory developments, update compliance programs, and engage with regulatory bodies to understand future requirements.

Conclusion

Preparing for the future of cybersecurity requires a forward-thinking approach, proactive strategies, and continuous adaptation to new challenges and opportunities. By understanding emerging trends, adopting proactive strategies, building a resilient security posture, and future-proofing cybersecurity efforts, organizations can enhance their security capabilities and stay ahead in the evolving cybersecurity landscape. This chapter provides valuable insights and practical guidance for preparing for the future of cybersecurity, offering a comprehensive approach to addressing the dynamic and ever-changing threats of the digital world. As technology continues to advance, the importance of staying informed, adaptive, and proactive in safeguarding digital assets cannot be overstated.

CHAPTER 31: CYBERSECURITY IN THE ERA OF DIGITAL TRANSFORMATION

Introduction

Digital transformation is reshaping industries and driving innovation by integrating digital technologies into all aspects of business operations. This transformation enhances efficiency, agility, and customer experiences, but it also introduces new cybersecurity challenges and risks. As organizations embrace digital transformation, ensuring robust cybersecurity measures is essential to protect digital assets, maintain trust, and support continuous innovation. This chapter explores the intersection of cybersecurity and digital transformation, the challenges and opportunities it presents, and strategies for building a secure digital future.

The Role of Cybersecurity in Digital Transformation

Cybersecurity plays a critical role in the success of digital transformation initiatives. Key aspects of this role include:

1. **Protecting Digital Assets:**
   - **Description:** As organizations digitize their operations, they generate and store vast amounts of data, including sensitive customer information, intellectual property,

and proprietary data. Protecting these digital assets from cyber threats is paramount.

- **Impact:** Data breaches, loss of intellectual property, financial losses, and reputational damage.

2. **Ensuring Business Continuity:**
   - **Description:** Digital transformation often involves the adoption of new technologies and processes that are integral to business operations. Ensuring the resilience and availability of these technologies is essential for business continuity.
   - **Impact:** Disruption of services, operational downtime, and loss of revenue.

3. **Compliance and Regulatory Requirements:**
   - **Description:** Digital transformation initiatives must comply with various cybersecurity and data protection regulations. Ensuring compliance is crucial to avoid legal penalties and maintain customer trust.
   - **Impact:** Regulatory fines, legal liabilities, and loss of customer trust.

4. **Building Customer Trust:**
   - **Description:** Customers expect their data to be protected and their privacy respected. Implementing robust cybersecurity measures is essential to building and maintaining customer trust.
   - **Impact:** Customer loyalty, brand reputation, and competitive advantage.

Cybersecurity Challenges in Digital Transformation

Digital transformation introduces several cybersecurity

challenges that organizations must address to protect their digital assets. Key challenges include:

1. **Increased Attack Surface:**
   - **Description:** Digital transformation expands the attack surface by introducing new technologies, devices, and interconnected systems. This creates more entry points for cyberattacks.
   - **Impact:** Increased risk of cyberattacks, potential for widespread disruptions, and difficulty in monitoring and securing all endpoints.

2. **Complex IT Environments:**
   - **Description:** Digital transformation often involves integrating legacy systems with new technologies, creating complex IT environments that can be difficult to secure.
   - **Impact:** Increased potential for vulnerabilities, challenges in implementing consistent security measures, and potential for security gaps.

3. **Shadow IT:**
   - **Description:** Employees may adopt new technologies and cloud services without the knowledge or approval of the IT department, known as shadow IT. This can introduce security risks and compliance issues.
   - **Impact:** Unauthorized access to sensitive data, lack of visibility into technology usage, and potential for data breaches.

4. **Third-Party Risks:**
   - **Description:** Digital transformation initiatives often involve collaboration with

third-party vendors and service providers. Ensuring the security of third-party relationships is critical.

- ○ **Impact:** Data breaches, unauthorized access, and supply chain attacks.

5. **Rapid Technology Adoption:**

- ○ **Description:** The rapid adoption of new technologies can outpace the implementation of security measures, creating potential vulnerabilities.
- ○ **Impact:** Increased risk of cyberattacks, challenges in keeping up with evolving threats, and potential for security gaps.

Strategies for Securing Digital Transformation

To address these challenges and ensure the security of digital transformation initiatives, organizations should implement a comprehensive set of strategies. Key strategies include:

1. **Implement a Zero Trust Architecture:**

- ○ **Description:** Adopt a Zero Trust security model that assumes no entity, whether inside or outside the network, is inherently trustworthy. Continuously verify every access request and enforce the principle of least privilege.
- ○ **Practices:** Use multi-factor authentication (MFA), implement micro-segmentation, enforce least privilege access, and monitor all network activities.

2. **Enhance Threat Detection and Response:**

- ○ **Description:** Implement advanced threat detection and response capabilities to identify and mitigate cyber threats in real-time.
- ○ **Practices:** Use security information and

event management (SIEM) solutions, deploy endpoint detection and response (EDR) tools, implement automated threat detection and response, and use machine learning for anomaly detection.

3. **Secure Cloud Environments:**
   - **Description:** Ensure the security of cloud environments by implementing cloud-native security solutions and best practices.
   - **Practices:** Use strong encryption for data at rest and in transit, implement access controls for cloud resources, continuously monitor cloud activities, and ensure compliance with cloud security standards.

4. **Conduct Security Assessments and Audits:**
   - **Description:** Perform regular security assessments and audits to identify vulnerabilities and assess the security posture of digital transformation initiatives.
   - **Practices:** Conduct vulnerability scans, penetration testing, and security audits, prioritize remediation efforts based on risk, and continuously monitor for new threats.

5. **Manage Third-Party Risks:**
   - **Description:** Assess the security practices of third-party vendors and service providers to ensure they meet the organization's cybersecurity standards.
   - **Practices:** Conduct due diligence, require security assessments and certifications, include security requirements in contracts, and monitor third-party activities for compliance.

6. **Foster a Culture of Cybersecurity:**

- ○ **Description:** Promote a culture of cybersecurity within the organization by raising awareness, providing training, and encouraging responsible behaviors.
- ○ **Practices:** Conduct regular security awareness training, provide role-specific training for employees, simulate phishing exercises, and promote a culture of security awareness.

Building a Secure Digital Future

Building a secure digital future involves implementing strategies that ensure the resilience and security of digital transformation initiatives. Key strategies for building a secure digital future include:

1. **Adopt Agile Security Practices:**
   - ○ **Description:** Implement agile security practices that can adapt to changing threats and technological advancements.
   - ○ **Practices:** Use modular security architectures, adopt DevSecOps principles, integrate security into the software development lifecycle (SDLC), and continuously review and update security policies and procedures.

2. **Invest in Research and Development:**
   - ○ **Description:** Invest in research and development to explore new security technologies, methodologies, and best practices.
   - ○ **Practices:** Collaborate with academic institutions, support cybersecurity research initiatives, and stay informed about emerging technologies.

3. **Emphasize Cyber Resilience:**
   - ○ **Description:** Focus on building cyber

resilience to ensure that organizations can withstand and recover from cyber incidents.

- **Practices:** Implement resilience-focused security measures, conduct regular resilience assessments, and develop comprehensive recovery plans.

4. **Prepare for Regulatory Changes:**

- **Description:** Stay informed about regulatory changes and ensure compliance with evolving cybersecurity and data protection regulations.

- **Practices:** Monitor regulatory developments, update compliance programs, and engage with regulatory bodies to understand future requirements.

5. **Leverage Advanced Technologies:**

- **Description:** Leverage advanced technologies, such as AI, machine learning, and blockchain, to enhance cybersecurity capabilities and stay ahead of evolving threats.

- **Practices:** Invest in AI-powered security solutions, explore the use of blockchain for secure data transactions, and implement machine learning for predictive threat analytics.

Conclusion

Cybersecurity is a critical component of successful digital transformation initiatives. By understanding the challenges and opportunities presented by digital transformation and implementing proactive strategies and best practices, organizations can enhance their cybersecurity posture and build a secure digital future. This chapter provides valuable insights and practical guidance for securing digital transformation, offering a comprehensive approach to addressing the evolving cybersecurity landscape. As organizations continue to embrace digital transformation, the importance of robust cybersecurity measures in protecting digital assets, ensuring business continuity, and supporting continuous innovation cannot be overstated.

CHAPTER 32: THE IMPORTANCE OF CYBERSECURITY LEADERSHIP

Introduction

Effective cybersecurity leadership is crucial for safeguarding an organization's digital assets, ensuring compliance with regulatory requirements, and fostering a culture of security. As cyber threats continue to evolve and grow in sophistication, strong leadership is essential to navigate the complexities of the cybersecurity landscape and drive strategic initiatives. This chapter explores the key roles and responsibilities of cybersecurity leaders, the qualities of effective cybersecurity leadership, and strategies for developing and nurturing cybersecurity leaders within an organization.

Key Roles and Responsibilities of Cybersecurity Leaders

Cybersecurity leaders play a vital role in shaping and implementing an organization's cybersecurity strategy. Key roles and responsibilities include:

1. **Chief Information Security Officer (CISO):**
   - **Description:** The CISO is a senior executive responsible for overseeing the organization's information security program. The CISO leads the security team, develops security policies,

and ensures compliance with regulatory requirements.

- **Responsibilities:** Develop and implement the cybersecurity strategy, manage security budgets, lead security teams, communicate with stakeholders about security risks and initiatives, and ensure regulatory compliance.

2. **Security Operations Manager:**
   - **Description:** The Security Operations Manager oversees the day-to-day operations of the security operations center (SOC). This role involves managing security analysts, monitoring security incidents, and coordinating incident response activities.
   - **Responsibilities:** Monitor security alerts, manage incident response, conduct threat analysis, coordinate with IT teams, and maintain security tools and technologies.

3. **Risk Management Leader:**
   - **Description:** The Risk Management Leader is responsible for identifying, assessing, and mitigating cybersecurity risks. This role involves developing risk management frameworks, conducting risk assessments, and implementing risk mitigation strategies.
   - **Responsibilities:** Identify and evaluate cybersecurity risks, develop risk management policies, implement risk mitigation measures, conduct regular risk assessments, and report on risk management activities.

4. **Compliance and Governance Leader:**
   - **Description:** The Compliance and Governance Leader ensures that the organization's cybersecurity practices align with regulatory

requirements and industry standards. This role involves developing compliance programs, conducting audits, and managing governance frameworks.

- **Responsibilities:** Develop and maintain compliance programs, conduct internal audits, ensure adherence to regulatory requirements, manage security policies and procedures, and report on compliance status.

Qualities of Effective Cybersecurity Leadership

Effective cybersecurity leadership requires a combination of technical expertise, strategic thinking, and interpersonal skills. Key qualities of effective cybersecurity leaders include:

1. **Visionary Thinking:**
   - **Description:** Cybersecurity leaders must be able to envision the future of cybersecurity, anticipate emerging threats, and develop forward-thinking strategies.
   - **Qualities:** Strategic planning, foresight, ability to align security initiatives with business goals.

2. **Technical Expertise:**
   - **Description:** A deep understanding of cybersecurity principles, technologies, and best practices is essential for effective leadership. Cybersecurity leaders must stay informed about the latest trends and developments in the field.
   - **Qualities:** Strong technical knowledge, continuous learning, ability to evaluate and implement security technologies.

3. **Communication Skills:**
   - **Description:** Effective communication is

critical for conveying the importance of cybersecurity to stakeholders, building support for security initiatives, and fostering a culture of security.

- **Qualities:** Clear and concise communication, ability to explain complex technical concepts to non-technical audiences, strong presentation skills.

4. **Decision-Making:**

- **Description:** Cybersecurity leaders must be able to make informed and timely decisions, especially in response to security incidents. This requires the ability to analyze data, assess risks, and weigh potential outcomes.

- **Qualities:** Analytical thinking, problem-solving, decisiveness, ability to handle pressure.

5. **Collaboration and Team Building:**

- **Description:** Building and leading effective cybersecurity teams requires strong collaboration and team-building skills. Cybersecurity leaders must foster a positive and inclusive work environment.

- **Qualities:** Team leadership, conflict resolution, ability to motivate and inspire team members, fostering a culture of collaboration.

6. **Ethical Integrity:**

- **Description:** Cybersecurity leaders must adhere to the highest standards of ethical conduct, ensuring that security practices align with legal and ethical guidelines.

- **Qualities:** Integrity, accountability, commitment to ethical principles, ability to set a positive example.

Strategies for Developing Cybersecurity Leaders

Organizations can develop and nurture cybersecurity leaders by implementing targeted strategies that support leadership development. Key strategies include:

1. **Professional Development and Training:**
   - **Description:** Provide opportunities for cybersecurity professionals to enhance their skills and knowledge through training programs, certifications, and continuous learning.
   - **Practices:** Offer access to cybersecurity courses and certifications (e.g., CISSP, CISM), support attendance at industry conferences and workshops, provide mentorship and coaching programs.

2. **Leadership Development Programs:**
   - **Description:** Implement leadership development programs that focus on building the skills and qualities necessary for effective cybersecurity leadership.
   - **Practices:** Develop tailored leadership training modules, create rotational programs that expose professionals to different aspects of cybersecurity, offer executive education programs.

3. **Career Pathways and Advancement:**
   - **Description:** Establish clear career pathways for cybersecurity professionals, providing opportunities for advancement and leadership roles.
   - **Practices:** Define career progression plans, create a framework for skills and competency

development, provide opportunities for lateral moves and cross-functional experiences.

4. **Encouraging Innovation and Initiative:**

   - **Description:** Foster an environment that encourages innovation and proactive problem-solving. Empower cybersecurity professionals to take initiative and lead security projects.

   - **Practices:** Create innovation labs and hackathons, support research and development initiatives, recognize and reward innovative solutions and contributions.

5. **Building a Supportive Culture:**

   - **Description:** Cultivate a supportive culture that values diversity, inclusion, and collaboration. Ensure that cybersecurity leaders have the resources and support needed to succeed.

   - **Practices:** Promote diversity and inclusion initiatives, provide access to mental health and well-being resources, create a positive and inclusive work environment.

Conclusion

Effective cybersecurity leadership is essential for safeguarding an organization's digital assets, navigating the complexities of the cybersecurity landscape, and fostering a culture of security. By understanding the key roles and responsibilities of cybersecurity leaders, recognizing the qualities of effective leadership, and implementing targeted strategies for leadership development, organizations can build and nurture a strong cadre of cybersecurity leaders. This chapter provides valuable insights and practical guidance for developing cybersecurity leadership, offering a comprehensive approach to building a secure and resilient organization. As cyber threats continue to evolve, the importance of strong and visionary cybersecurity leadership in protecting digital assets and ensuring business continuity cannot be overstated.

CHAPTER 33: NAVIGATING CYBERSECURITY IN A POST-PANDEMIC WORLD

Introduction

The COVID-19 pandemic has accelerated the adoption of digital technologies and remote work, transforming the way organizations operate. While these changes have enabled business continuity and innovation, they have also introduced new cybersecurity challenges. As the world transitions to a post-pandemic era, it is essential for organizations to navigate the evolving cybersecurity landscape and adapt their strategies to address emerging threats and vulnerabilities. This chapter explores the impact of the pandemic on cybersecurity, the key challenges faced in a post-pandemic world, and strategies for building a resilient cybersecurity posture.

Impact of the Pandemic on Cybersecurity

The pandemic has had a profound impact on cybersecurity, driven by several key factors:

1. **Remote Work and Telecommuting:**
   ◦ **Description:** The rapid shift to remote work and telecommuting has expanded the

attack surface, as employees access corporate resources from various locations and devices.

- **Impact:** Increased risk of cyberattacks, potential for insecure remote access, and challenges in monitoring and securing remote work environments.

2. **Increased Use of Cloud Services:**

- **Description:** Organizations have accelerated their adoption of cloud services to support remote work, collaboration, and digital transformation.

- **Impact:** Greater reliance on cloud security, potential for misconfigurations, and the need for robust data protection measures.

3. **Rise in Phishing and Social Engineering Attacks:**

- **Description:** Cybercriminals have exploited the uncertainty and fear surrounding the pandemic to launch phishing and social engineering attacks.

- **Impact:** Increased susceptibility to phishing, potential for credential theft, and heightened need for security awareness.

4. **Shift in IT Priorities:**

- **Description:** Organizations have had to rapidly adjust their IT priorities to support remote work and digital initiatives, sometimes at the expense of cybersecurity.

- **Impact:** Potential for security gaps, increased risk of vulnerabilities, and need for ongoing security assessments.

Key Cybersecurity Challenges in a Post-Pandemic World

As organizations navigate the post-pandemic world, they face several key cybersecurity challenges:

1. **Securing Hybrid Work Environments:**
   - **Description:** The hybrid work model, which combines remote and on-site work, presents unique security challenges as employees move between different work environments.
   - **Impact:** Need for flexible and adaptive security measures, potential for inconsistent security practices, and challenges in securing diverse endpoints.

2. **Managing Supply Chain Risks:**
   - **Description:** The increased reliance on third-party vendors and service providers during the pandemic has heightened supply chain risks.
   - **Impact:** Potential for supply chain attacks, need for robust vendor risk management, and importance of continuous monitoring.

3. **Addressing Insider Threats:**
   - **Description:** The stress and uncertainty caused by the pandemic may increase the risk of insider threats, as employees face new challenges and pressures.
   - **Impact:** Need for enhanced monitoring of user behavior, implementation of insider threat programs, and fostering a supportive work culture.

4. **Ensuring Regulatory Compliance:**
   - **Description:** Organizations must navigate evolving regulatory requirements and ensure compliance with data protection and cybersecurity regulations.
   - **Impact:** Resource-intensive compliance efforts, need for continuous monitoring and

reporting, and challenges in keeping up with regulatory changes.

Strategies for Building a Resilient Cybersecurity Posture

To address these challenges and build a resilient cybersecurity posture, organizations should implement a comprehensive set of strategies. Key strategies include:

1. **Implement Zero Trust Security:**
   - **Description:** Adopt a Zero Trust security model that assumes no entity, whether inside or outside the network, is inherently trustworthy. Continuously verify every access request and enforce the principle of least privilege.
   - **Practices:** Use multi-factor authentication (MFA), implement micro-segmentation, enforce least privilege access, and monitor all network activities.

2. **Enhance Remote Work Security:**
   - **Description:** Strengthen security measures for remote work environments to protect against cyber threats and ensure secure access to corporate resources.
   - **Practices:** Use virtual private networks (VPNs), implement endpoint protection, conduct regular security training for remote workers, and ensure secure configurations for remote access tools.

3. **Strengthen Cloud Security:**
   - **Description:** Ensure the security of cloud environments by implementing cloud-native security solutions and best practices.
   - **Practices:** Use strong encryption for data at rest and in transit, implement access controls

for cloud resources, continuously monitor cloud activities, and ensure compliance with cloud security standards.

4. **Conduct Regular Security Assessments:**
   - **Description:** Perform regular security assessments to identify vulnerabilities and assess the security posture of the organization's IT environment.
   - **Practices:** Conduct vulnerability scans, penetration testing, and security audits, prioritize remediation efforts based on risk, and continuously monitor for new threats.

5. **Develop a Comprehensive Incident Response Plan:**
   - **Description:** Establish an incident response plan to effectively manage and mitigate cybersecurity incidents. A well-defined plan ensures a coordinated and timely response to cyber threats.
   - **Practices:** Define roles and responsibilities, establish communication protocols, conduct incident response drills, and document incident response procedures.

6. **Foster a Culture of Cybersecurity:**
   - **Description:** Promote a culture of cybersecurity within the organization by raising awareness, providing training, and encouraging responsible behaviors.
   - **Practices:** Conduct regular security awareness training, provide role-specific training for employees, simulate phishing exercises, and promote a culture of security awareness.

Embracing Innovation in Cybersecurity

Embracing innovation in cybersecurity is essential to stay ahead of evolving threats and enhance the organization's security posture. Key considerations for embracing innovation include:

1. **Leveraging Advanced Technologies:**
   - **Description:** Utilize advanced technologies, such as artificial intelligence (AI), machine learning (ML), and blockchain, to enhance cybersecurity capabilities.
   - **Practices:** Invest in AI-powered security solutions, explore the use of blockchain for secure data transactions, and implement ML for predictive threat analytics.

2. **Adopting Agile Security Practices:**
   - **Description:** Implement agile security practices that can adapt to changing threats and technological advancements.
   - **Practices:** Use modular security architectures, adopt DevSecOps principles, integrate security into the software development lifecycle (SDLC), and continuously review and update security policies and procedures.

3. **Collaborating with Industry Partners:**
   - **Description:** Foster collaboration with industry partners, government agencies, and cybersecurity communities to share threat intelligence and best practices.
   - **Practices:** Participate in information-sharing networks, engage in public-private partnerships, and collaborate on joint cybersecurity initiatives.

4. **Investing in Research and Development:**
   - **Description:** Invest in research and development to explore new security technologies, methodologies, and best

practices.

○ **Practices:** Collaborate with academic institutions, support cybersecurity research initiatives, and stay informed about emerging technologies.

Conclusion

The post-pandemic world presents new cybersecurity challenges and opportunities. By understanding the impact of the pandemic on cybersecurity, addressing key challenges, and implementing proactive strategies, organizations can build a resilient cybersecurity posture that supports business continuity and innovation. This chapter provides valuable insights and practical guidance for navigating cybersecurity in a post-pandemic world, offering a comprehensive approach to addressing the evolving cybersecurity landscape. As organizations continue to adapt to the new normal, the importance of robust cybersecurity measures in protecting digital assets, ensuring business continuity, and fostering a culture of security cannot be overstated.

CHAPTER 34: CYBERSECURITY IN THE AGE OF ARTIFICIAL INTELLIGENCE AND MACHINE LEARNING

Introduction

As artificial intelligence (AI) and machine learning (ML) continue to advance, their integration into various industries is revolutionizing the way organizations operate. While these technologies offer significant benefits, they also introduce new cybersecurity challenges and opportunities. Ensuring the security of AI and ML systems is crucial to protect digital assets, maintain trust, and support continuous innovation. This chapter explores the intersection of cybersecurity and AI/ML, the challenges and risks associated with these technologies, and strategies for building secure and resilient AI/ML systems.

The Role of AI and ML in Cybersecurity

AI and ML are playing an increasingly important role in enhancing cybersecurity measures. Key applications of AI and ML in cybersecurity include:

1. **Threat Detection and Analysis:**

- **Description:** AI and ML algorithms can analyze vast amounts of data to identify patterns and anomalies indicative of cyber threats. These technologies can detect previously unknown threats by recognizing unusual behaviors.
- **Applications:** Intrusion detection systems (IDS), security information and event management (SIEM) solutions, endpoint detection and response (EDR) tools, network traffic analysis.

2. **Behavioral Analytics:**

- **Description:** AI can analyze user behavior to establish baselines of normal activity and identify deviations that may indicate malicious activity. Behavioral analytics helps detect insider threats and compromised accounts.
- **Applications:** User and entity behavior analytics (UEBA), fraud detection systems, anomaly detection in authentication and access patterns.

3. **Automated Incident Response:**

- **Description:** AI-powered systems can automate incident response processes, enabling rapid and efficient handling of security incidents. Automated response can include actions such as isolating affected systems, blocking malicious traffic, and notifying relevant personnel.
- **Applications:** Security orchestration, automation, and response (SOAR) platforms, automated malware analysis, real-time threat mitigation.

4. **Vulnerability Management:**

   ◦ **Description:** AI can assist in identifying and prioritizing vulnerabilities based on risk, helping organizations focus their remediation efforts on the most critical issues.

   ◦ **Applications:** Vulnerability scanning and assessment tools, predictive vulnerability analytics, automated patch management.

5. **Phishing Detection and Prevention:**

   ◦ **Description:** AI can analyze email content and sender behavior to detect phishing attempts and prevent them from reaching end-users.

   ◦ **Applications:** Email security gateways, anti-phishing tools, real-time phishing detection systems.

Challenges and Risks of AI and ML in Cybersecurity

While AI and ML offer numerous benefits, they also present challenges and risks that must be addressed to ensure their effective and secure use:

1. **Adversarial Attacks:**

   ◦ **Description:** Attackers can manipulate AI models by introducing malicious inputs designed to deceive the system and evade detection. Adversarial attacks pose a significant threat to AI-driven security solutions.

   ◦ **Challenges:** Developing robust defenses against adversarial attacks, implementing techniques for adversarial training, ensuring model resilience.

2. **Data Quality and Bias:**

   ◦ **Description:** AI models rely on high-quality data for training and analysis. Incomplete, biased, or inaccurate data can lead to flawed models and erroneous results.

- **Challenges:** Ensuring access to diverse and comprehensive datasets, addressing data quality issues, mitigating biases in data.

3. **Model Interpretability:**

- **Description:** Complex AI models, particularly deep learning models, can be difficult to interpret and understand. Lack of transparency in AI decision-making can hinder trust and accountability.

- **Challenges:** Improving model interpretability, providing explanations for AI decisions, ensuring transparency in AI-driven security processes.

4. **Resource Requirements:**

- **Description:** Training and deploying AI models can require significant computational resources and expertise. Smaller organizations may struggle to implement and maintain AI-driven security solutions.

- **Challenges:** Addressing resource constraints, providing access to scalable and cost-effective AI solutions, offering training and support for AI implementation.

5. **Ethical and Privacy Considerations:**

- **Description:** The use of AI in cybersecurity raises ethical and privacy concerns, particularly regarding the collection and analysis of sensitive data. Ensuring ethical AI practices is essential for maintaining trust and compliance.

- **Challenges:** Implementing privacy-preserving AI techniques, ensuring ethical AI usage, adhering to regulatory requirements.

Strategies for Building Secure AI and ML Systems

To address these challenges and ensure the security and resilience of AI and ML systems, organizations should implement a comprehensive set of strategies. Key strategies include:

1. **Adversarial Robustness:**
   - **Description:** Ensure that AI models are robust against adversarial attacks, where malicious inputs are crafted to deceive the model and produce incorrect outputs.
   - **Practices:** Use adversarial training, implement input validation, and employ defensive distillation techniques.

2. **Data Quality and Integrity:**
   - **Description:** Ensure the quality and integrity of data used to train AI models to prevent data poisoning and unauthorized access.
   - **Practices:** Use differential privacy techniques, implement access controls for training data, and monitor data usage.

3. **Model Explainability:**
   - **Description:** Ensure that AI models are interpretable and explainable to allow for better understanding and verification of their decision-making processes.
   - **Practices:** Use explainable AI techniques, provide transparency reports, and involve domain experts in model validation.

4. **Secure Deployment and Monitoring:**
   - **Description:** Securely deploy AI models to prevent unauthorized access and tampering. Use continuous monitoring to detect

anomalies and ensure the ongoing security of deployed models.

- ◦ **Practices:** Implement access controls, use containerization and sandboxing, verify the integrity of deployed models, and continuously monitor for signs of compromise.

5. **Ethical and Privacy Considerations:**

   - ◦ **Description:** Ensure that AI systems are designed and deployed ethically, considering potential biases and ensuring fairness and accountability.

   - ◦ **Practices:** Conduct ethical reviews, implement fairness metrics, and involve diverse teams in the development and evaluation of AI models.

Future Trends in AI and ML for Cybersecurity

The future of AI and ML in cybersecurity is shaped by ongoing advancements in technology and evolving threat landscapes. Key trends to watch for include:

1. **Federated Learning and Privacy-Preserving AI:**

   - ◦ **Description:** Federated learning enables the training of AI models on decentralized data sources without sharing sensitive data. Privacy-preserving AI techniques will ensure that data privacy is maintained while leveraging AI capabilities.

   - ◦ **Future Impact:** Increased adoption of privacy-preserving AI, improved data security, broader access to AI-driven security solutions.

2. **AI-Powered Threat Intelligence:**

   - ◦ **Description:** The integration of AI with threat intelligence platforms will enable more accurate and timely analysis of threat data, providing organizations with actionable insights for proactive defense.

- **Future Impact:** Enhanced threat intelligence capabilities, improved anticipation of emerging threats, better-informed security strategies.

3. **Human-AI Collaboration:**

- **Description:** AI-driven security solutions will increasingly complement human expertise, with AI handling routine tasks and humans focusing on complex decision-making and strategic planning.
- **Future Impact:** Improved synergy between AI and human analysts, enhanced overall security effectiveness, reduced workload for security teams.

4. **Quantum-Resistant AI:**

- **Description:** The development of AI-driven security solutions that are resistant to quantum computing threats will be essential as quantum technologies become more advanced.
- **Future Impact:** Improved resilience against quantum-based attacks, enhanced long-term security, better preparation for future technological advancements.

5. **AI for IoT Security:**

- **Description:** As the Internet of Things (IoT) continues to grow, AI-driven security solutions will play a crucial role in protecting IoT devices and networks from cyber threats.
- **Future Impact:** Enhanced IoT security, improved threat detection and response for

connected devices, greater resilience against IoT-specific threats.

Conclusion

The integration of AI and ML into cybersecurity is revolutionizing the way organizations protect their digital assets. By understanding the challenges and risks associated with these technologies and implementing proactive strategies and best practices, organizations can build secure and resilient AI/ML systems. This chapter provides valuable insights and practical guidance for navigating the intersection of cybersecurity and AI/ML, offering a comprehensive approach to addressing the evolving cybersecurity landscape. As AI and ML continue to advance, their integration into cybersecurity will be essential for building a resilient and secure digital future.

CHAPTER 35:
CYBERSECURITY
AND BLOCKCHAIN
TECHNOLOGY

Introduction

Blockchain technology, known for its role in cryptocurrencies like Bitcoin, has the potential to revolutionize various industries by providing secure, transparent, and decentralized systems. While blockchain offers significant benefits, it also introduces new cybersecurity challenges and opportunities. Ensuring the security of blockchain implementations is essential to protect digital assets, maintain trust, and support continuous innovation. This chapter explores the intersection of cybersecurity and blockchain technology, the challenges and risks associated with blockchain, and strategies for building secure and resilient blockchain systems.

The Role of Blockchain in Cybersecurity

Blockchain technology can enhance cybersecurity in several ways by providing secure and tamper-resistant systems. Key applications of blockchain in cybersecurity include:

1. **Data Integrity and Verification:**
     ◦ **Description:** Blockchain's decentralized and immutable nature ensures that data stored on the blockchain cannot be altered or tampered

with. This enhances data integrity and provides a reliable verification mechanism.

- ◦ **Applications:** Secure record-keeping, supply chain traceability, and data integrity verification for critical systems.

2. **Decentralized Identity Management:**

- ◦ **Description:** Blockchain can be used to create decentralized and tamper-proof digital identities. This enhances the security of identity verification and access management processes.

- ◦ **Applications:** Decentralized identity platforms, secure authentication systems, and self-sovereign identity solutions.

3. **Smart Contracts:**

- ◦ **Description:** Smart contracts are self-executing contracts with the terms of the agreement directly written into code. They automatically execute and enforce the terms without the need for intermediaries.

- ◦ **Applications:** Automated financial transactions, supply chain automation, and secure digital agreements.

4. **Secure Data Sharing:**

- ◦ **Description:** Blockchain enables secure and transparent data sharing between parties without the need for a central authority. This enhances data security and trust in data exchange processes.

- ◦ **Applications:** Secure data sharing in healthcare, financial services, and government.

5. **Cryptographic Security:**

- **Description:** Blockchain relies on cryptographic algorithms to secure transactions and data. This enhances the overall security of blockchain systems and protects against unauthorized access.
- **Applications:** Cryptographic hash functions, public key infrastructure (PKI), and digital signatures.

Challenges and Risks of Blockchain Technology

While blockchain offers numerous benefits, it also presents challenges and risks that must be addressed to ensure its effective and secure use:

1. **Scalability:**
   - **Description:** Blockchain networks can face scalability issues as the number of transactions and participants increases. This can impact the performance and efficiency of the blockchain.
   - **Challenges:** Implementing scalable consensus mechanisms, optimizing transaction processing, and addressing network congestion.

2. **Consensus Mechanisms:**
   - **Description:** Blockchain relies on consensus mechanisms to validate transactions and maintain the integrity of the ledger. Different consensus mechanisms have varying levels of security and efficiency.
   - **Challenges:** Selecting appropriate consensus mechanisms, addressing the energy consumption of proof-of-work (PoW), and ensuring the security of proof-of-stake (PoS) systems.

3. **Smart Contract Security:**

- **Description:** Smart contracts are susceptible to vulnerabilities and coding errors that can be exploited by attackers. Ensuring the security of smart contracts is critical to prevent financial losses and unauthorized actions.
- **Challenges:** Conducting thorough code reviews, using formal verification methods, and implementing secure coding practices.

4. **Privacy Concerns:**

- **Description:** While blockchain provides transparency, it can also raise privacy concerns as transaction data is publicly accessible. Balancing transparency with privacy is a significant challenge.
- **Challenges:** Implementing privacy-preserving techniques, using zero-knowledge proofs, and ensuring data confidentiality.

5. **Regulatory and Compliance Issues:**

- **Description:** The regulatory landscape for blockchain and cryptocurrencies is still evolving. Ensuring compliance with relevant regulations and standards is essential for legal and operational stability.
- **Challenges:** Navigating regulatory requirements, ensuring compliance with anti-money laundering (AML) and know-your-customer (KYC) regulations, and adapting to changing legal frameworks.

Strategies for Building Secure Blockchain Systems

To address these challenges and ensure the security and resilience of blockchain systems, organizations should implement a comprehensive set of strategies. Key strategies include:

1. **Selecting Appropriate Consensus Mechanisms:**
   - **Description:** Choose consensus mechanisms that balance security, scalability, and efficiency based on the specific use case and network requirements.
   - **Practices:** Evaluate different consensus mechanisms (e.g., PoW, PoS, Delegated Proof of Stake), consider hybrid approaches, and ensure robust security measures.

2. **Implementing Smart Contract Security:**
   - **Description:** Ensure that smart contracts are secure and free from vulnerabilities that could be exploited by attackers.
   - **Practices:** Conduct thorough code reviews, use formal verification methods, implement secure coding practices, and conduct regular security audits.

3. **Enhancing Data Privacy:**
   - **Description:** Implement privacy-preserving techniques to protect sensitive data while maintaining the benefits of blockchain transparency.
   - **Practices:** Use zero-knowledge proofs, implement privacy-enhancing technologies (e.g., zk-SNARKs, confidential transactions), and consider off-chain data storage solutions.

4. **Ensuring Regulatory Compliance:**
   - **Description:** Ensure that blockchain implementations comply with relevant regulations and standards to maintain legal and operational stability.

      ○ **Practices:** Stay informed about regulatory developments, implement AML and KYC measures, and ensure compliance with data protection regulations (e.g., GDPR).

5. **Conducting Regular Security Assessments:**

      ○ **Description:** Perform regular security assessments to identify vulnerabilities and assess the security posture of blockchain systems.

      ○ **Practices:** Conduct vulnerability scans, penetration testing, and security audits, prioritize remediation efforts based on risk, and continuously monitor for new threats.

Future Trends in Blockchain and Cybersecurity

The future of blockchain and cybersecurity is shaped by ongoing advancements in technology and evolving threat landscapes. Key trends to watch for include:

1. **Interoperability and Integration:**

      ○ **Description:** The development of interoperable blockchain platforms that can communicate and integrate with each other will enhance the scalability and functionality of blockchain systems.

      ○ **Future Impact:** Improved cross-chain communication, greater flexibility in blockchain applications, enhanced security through shared protocols.

2. **Blockchain for Supply Chain Security:**

      ○ **Description:** Blockchain technology will play a crucial role in enhancing supply chain security by providing transparent and tamper-proof records of product origins and movements.

○ **Future Impact:** Enhanced traceability, reduced risk of counterfeit products, improved supply chain integrity.

3. **Decentralized Finance (DeFi) Security:**

   ○ **Description:** The rise of decentralized finance (DeFi) platforms introduces new security challenges and opportunities. Ensuring the security of DeFi applications is essential for their success.

   ○ **Future Impact:** Improved security measures for DeFi platforms, increased adoption of decentralized financial services, enhanced financial inclusion.

4. **Blockchain for Identity Management:**

   ○ **Description:** Blockchain technology will continue to advance decentralized identity management solutions, providing secure and tamper-proof digital identities.

   ○ **Future Impact:** Improved identity verification processes, enhanced privacy and control over personal data, greater trust in digital identity systems.

5. **Quantum-Resistant Blockchain:**

   ○ **Description:** The development of quantum-resistant blockchain technologies will be essential as quantum computing becomes more advanced.

   ○ **Future Impact:** Enhanced resilience against quantum-based attacks, improved long-term security, better preparation for future technological advancements.

Conclusion

Blockchain technology offers significant benefits for

enhancing cybersecurity by providing secure, transparent, and decentralized systems. By understanding the challenges and risks associated with blockchain and implementing proactive strategies and best practices, organizations can build secure and resilient blockchain systems. This chapter provides valuable insights and practical guidance for navigating the intersection of cybersecurity and blockchain technology, offering a comprehensive approach to addressing the evolving cybersecurity landscape. As blockchain technology continues to advance, its integration into cybersecurity will be essential for building a resilient and secure digital future.

CHAPTER 36: THE INTERSECTION OF CYBERSECURITY AND ARTIFICIAL INTELLIGENCE ETHICS

Introduction

The integration of artificial intelligence (AI) in cybersecurity has brought about significant advancements in threat detection, analysis, and response. However, the use of AI in cybersecurity also raises important ethical considerations. Ensuring that AI-driven security solutions are developed and deployed responsibly is crucial to maintaining trust, protecting privacy, and ensuring fairness. This chapter explores the ethical implications of using AI in cybersecurity, the potential risks and challenges, and strategies for promoting ethical AI practices.

Ethical Implications of AI in Cybersecurity

The use of AI in cybersecurity presents several ethical implications that must be carefully considered:

1. **Bias and Fairness:**
    - **Description:** AI models can inherit biases present in the training data, leading to unfair or discriminatory outcomes. Ensuring fairness and mitigating bias is essential to

building ethical AI systems.

- ◦ **Implications:** Potential for biased threat detection, unfair treatment of individuals or groups, and loss of trust in AI-driven security solutions.

2. **Privacy Concerns:**

- ◦ **Description:** AI-driven cybersecurity solutions often require access to large amounts of data, including sensitive personal information. Protecting privacy and ensuring data security are critical ethical considerations.
- ◦ **Implications:** Risk of data breaches, unauthorized access to personal information, and potential violations of privacy rights.

3. **Transparency and Accountability:**

- ◦ **Description:** The complexity of AI models can make it difficult to understand how decisions are made. Ensuring transparency and accountability in AI-driven cybersecurity is essential to maintain trust and credibility.
- ◦ **Implications:** Lack of transparency in decision-making processes, challenges in explaining AI-driven actions, and potential for accountability gaps.

4. **Autonomy and Control:**

- ◦ **Description:** AI systems can operate autonomously, making decisions without human intervention. Balancing autonomy with human oversight is important to ensure ethical use of AI in cybersecurity.
- ◦ **Implications:** Potential for unintended consequences, loss of human control, and challenges in managing AI-driven actions.

Risks and Challenges of Ethical AI in Cybersecurity

Several risks and challenges must be addressed to ensure the ethical use of AI in cybersecurity:

1. **Data Quality and Bias Mitigation:**
   - **Description:** Ensuring the quality and diversity of training data is essential to mitigate bias and ensure fairness in AI models.
   - **Challenges:** Obtaining high-quality and representative data, addressing data quality issues, and implementing bias mitigation techniques.

2. **Privacy-Preserving AI Techniques:**
   - **Description:** Implementing privacy-preserving AI techniques is crucial to protect sensitive data and ensure compliance with data protection regulations.
   - **Challenges:** Balancing data access with privacy protection, implementing techniques such as differential privacy and federated learning, and ensuring data security.

3. **Explainability and Interpretability:**
   - **Description:** Improving the explainability and interpretability of AI models is essential to ensure transparency and build trust in AI-driven cybersecurity solutions.
   - **Challenges:** Developing techniques for explainable AI, providing clear explanations for AI-driven decisions, and ensuring transparency in decision-making processes.

4. **Ethical Governance and Regulation:**
   - **Description:** Establishing ethical governance frameworks and ensuring compliance with

relevant regulations are essential to promote responsible AI use in cybersecurity.

- **Challenges:** Developing and implementing ethical guidelines, ensuring compliance with regulatory requirements, and fostering a culture of ethical AI practices.

Strategies for Promoting Ethical AI Practices

To address these challenges and promote ethical AI practices in cybersecurity, organizations should implement a comprehensive set of strategies. Key strategies include:

1. **Bias Detection and Mitigation:**
   - **Description:** Implement techniques to detect and mitigate bias in AI models, ensuring fairness and reducing the potential for discriminatory outcomes.
   - **Practices:** Conduct bias audits, use fairness-aware machine learning algorithms, implement bias mitigation techniques, and continuously monitor for bias.

2. **Privacy-Preserving AI:**
   - **Description:** Implement privacy-preserving AI techniques to protect sensitive data and ensure compliance with data protection regulations.
   - **Practices:** Use differential privacy, implement federated learning, ensure data encryption, and minimize data collection and retention.

3. **Explainable AI:**
   - **Description:** Develop and implement techniques for explainable AI to provide clear and understandable explanations for AI-driven decisions.
   - **Practices:** Use model-agnostic explanation

methods, implement interpretable machine learning models, provide transparency reports, and involve domain experts in model validation.

4. **Ethical Governance Frameworks:**

  ◦ **Description:** Establish ethical governance frameworks to guide the development and deployment of AI-driven cybersecurity solutions.

  ◦ **Practices:** Develop ethical guidelines and principles, create ethics review boards, ensure compliance with regulatory requirements, and promote a culture of ethical AI practices.

5. **Human Oversight and Control:**

  ◦ **Description:** Ensure that AI-driven cybersecurity solutions operate with appropriate human oversight and control to prevent unintended consequences and maintain accountability.

  ◦ **Practices:** Implement human-in-the-loop systems, establish clear roles and responsibilities, conduct regular reviews and audits, and ensure human intervention in critical decision-making processes.

Future Trends in Ethical AI and Cybersecurity

The future of ethical AI in cybersecurity is shaped by ongoing advancements in technology and evolving ethical considerations. Key trends to watch for include:

1. **Advancements in Fairness and Bias Mitigation:**

  ◦ **Description:** Ongoing research and development in fairness-aware machine learning will lead to improved techniques for detecting and mitigating bias in AI models.

○ **Future Impact:** Enhanced fairness in AI-driven security solutions, reduced potential for discriminatory outcomes, increased trust in AI systems.

2. **Privacy-Preserving AI Techniques:**

   ○ **Description:** Continued advancements in privacy-preserving AI techniques will enable more secure and privacy-conscious data analysis and decision-making.

   ○ **Future Impact:** Improved data privacy and security, increased compliance with data protection regulations, broader adoption of privacy-preserving AI solutions.

3. **Explainable AI and Transparency:**

   ○ **Description:** The development of more sophisticated explainable AI techniques will enhance transparency and understanding of AI-driven decisions.

   ○ **Future Impact:** Greater trust and credibility in AI systems, improved accountability, better-informed decision-making.

4. **Ethical AI Governance:**

   ○ **Description:** The establishment of robust ethical AI governance frameworks will guide the responsible development and deployment of AI-driven cybersecurity solutions.

   ○ **Future Impact:** Increased adherence to ethical principles, improved regulatory compliance, strengthened culture of ethical AI practices.

5. **Collaboration and Stakeholder Engagement:**

   ○ **Description:** Collaboration between industry, academia, government, and other stakeholders will be essential to address ethical challenges and promote responsible AI use.

○ **Future Impact:** Enhanced collaboration and information-sharing, development of best practices, broader consensus on ethical AI standards.

Conclusion

The integration of AI in cybersecurity presents significant opportunities for enhancing threat detection, analysis, and response. However, it also raises important ethical considerations that must be addressed to ensure responsible and fair use of AI technologies. By understanding the ethical implications, addressing the challenges, and implementing proactive strategies, organizations can promote ethical AI practices and build trust in AI-driven cybersecurity solutions. This chapter provides valuable insights and practical guidance for navigating the intersection of cybersecurity and AI ethics, offering a comprehensive approach to addressing the evolving cybersecurity landscape. As AI continues to advance, the importance of ethical AI practices in protecting digital assets and ensuring fairness and accountability cannot be overstated.

ACKNOWLEDGEMENT

The completion of this book, "Complete Cybersecurity Expertise," would not have been possible without the invaluable contributions and support of many individuals and organizations. Their expertise, guidance, and encouragement have played a crucial role in shaping this comprehensive resource on cybersecurity.

First and foremost, we extend our heartfelt gratitude to the cybersecurity professionals and experts whose insights and experiences have enriched the content of this book. Their dedication to safeguarding digital assets and their unwavering commitment to advancing the field of cybersecurity are truly commendable.

We would like to thank the many researchers, academics, and thought leaders whose groundbreaking work and innovative ideas have informed and inspired the chapters within this book. Their contributions to the body of knowledge in cybersecurity continue to drive the industry forward and pave the way for new advancements.

Our deepest appreciation goes to the organizations and institutions that have supported this endeavor. Their commitment to cybersecurity education and their efforts to promote best practices and knowledge sharing have been instrumental in bringing this book to fruition.

We are also grateful to the reviewers and editors who have meticulously reviewed the content, providing valuable feedback and ensuring the highest standards of quality and accuracy. Their attention to detail and dedication to excellence have greatly enhanced the clarity and coherence of this book.

A special thank you to the educators and trainers who tirelessly work to impart cybersecurity knowledge and skills to the next generation of professionals. Their passion for teaching and their commitment to student success are vital to building a strong and capable cybersecurity workforce.

To our families, friends, and colleagues, we express our heartfelt thanks for their unwavering support, patience, and understanding throughout the writing process. Their encouragement and belief in the importance of this work have been a constant source of motivation.

Finally, we would like to acknowledge the readers of this book. Your curiosity, dedication to learning, and commitment to enhancing your cybersecurity expertise are what drive the continuous evolution of this field. We hope that this book serves as a valuable resource in your journey to becoming proficient in cybersecurity.

With deep gratitude,

Manuh

◆ ◆ ◆

.

www.ingramcontent.com/pod-product-compliance
Lightning Source LLC
LaVergne TN
LVHW051436050326
832903LV00030BD/3121